How to Know If It's Time to Go

✓
2010

How to Know If It's Time to Go

A 10-Step Reality Test for Your Marriage

Dr. Lawrence Birnbach
and Dr. Beverly Hyman

STERLING ETHOS
An imprint of Sterling Publishing Co., Inc.

New York / London
www.sterlingpublishing.com

STERLING and the distinctive Sterling logo are registered trademarks of
Sterling Publishing Co., Inc.

Library of Congress Cataloging-in-Publication Data
Birnbach, Lawrence.
How to know if it's time to go : a 10-step reality test for your marriage/Lawrence Birnbach, Beverly Hyman.
p. cm.
Includes index.
ISBN 978-1-4027-6643-5
1. Marriage. 2. Marriage--Psychological aspects. 3. Divorce. I. Hyman, Beverly. II. Title.
HQ734.B626 2010
306.89--dc22

2009031599

2 4 6 8 10 9 7 5 3 1

Published by Sterling Publishing Co., Inc.
387 Park Avenue South, New York, NY 10016

Distributed in Canada by Sterling Publishing
c/o Canadian Manda Group, 165 Dufferin Street
Toronto, Ontario, Canada M6K 3H6
Distributed in the United Kingdom by GMC Distribution Services
Castle Place, 166 High Street, Lewes, East Sussex, England BN7 1XU
Distributed in Australia by Capricorn Link (Australia) Pty. Ltd.
P.O. Box 704, Windsor, NSW 2756, Australia

Manufactured in the United States

Sterling ISBN 978-1-4027-6643-5

For information about custom editions, special sales, premium and
corporate purchases, please contact Sterling Special Sales Department
at 800-805-5489 or specialsales@sterlingpublishing.com.

To Marlo and Rachel:
Our love for you inspired us to ask the questions
that led us to write this book.

Authors' Disclaimer

The advice in this book is written from a general perspective. It is not meant to be specific to any reader's particular situation. It is most definitely not intended for any person to take specific action to end their marriage. It is intended to encourage the reader to recognize the issues that may be contributing to his or her problems, to discuss these with his or her spouse, and to seek professional assistance if it is indicated.

Many wise researchers agree that in researching the literature on marriage and divorce it is possible to find evidence that will support quite different points of view. We believe we have sincerely presented the current body of work reported by many of the most highly respected researchers in the field. Our emphasis is on what we believe to be the underreported parts of the research.

The people we write about in this book are all real. Their stories are true. The details have been altered to protect their anonymity.

"Learning to live with a person you do not love and respect, learning to live with a person who neither loves nor respects you, is merely learning how to die, how to walk around as a shell, how to deny how you feel, how to hate without showing it, how to weep without tears, how to declare that the sham you live is the true reality and that it is good."

—Jules Henry

CONTENTS

Acknowledgments

We thank our great friends Jutta Sayles and Jules Kramer, who believed in us and our project, even when we were faltering, and used their networking magic to connect us to the right people. You were the catalyst that made it happen. We thank Jane Wesman, President of Jane Wesman Public Relations, Inc., who recognized the project's potential and connected us to Al Zuckerman, our savvy and wise agent at Writers House. Thank you, Al, not only for selling the manuscript, but for first helping us to better understand the book we were trying to write. We thank our three editors at Sterling Publishing: Meredith Hale, for convincing Sterling to take the book and for her wonderful editorial input; Tricia Medved, for picking up where Meredith left off and contributing additional wonderful editorial support in her own right; and Barbara Clark, for ushering us through many important aspects of finishing a manuscript. We also thank the interviewees, patients, relatives, and friends who generously contributed their stories so that others might benefit from their openness. Your candor and your need to be understood invigorated us and reinforced for us that we were on the right track.

INTRODUCTION

Is This Me?

It was 3:30 a.m. when Ann looked at the clock next to her bed. The alarm was set for 6:30, but her sleep had ended, as it often did now. She lay quietly next to her sleeping husband. She had been dreaming of being locked in an empty house. The dream reminded her of her empty relationship and the growing sadness that she had felt during the last five years. She thought of the previous evening, the dinner she had cooked, and then waited to share with Frank, his kiss on her cheek when he came home at 8:00 o'clock, the meal they ate mostly in silence, followed by his quick retreat to the den to make business calls. She felt like crying, but only let out a sigh so as not to wake him. He was irritable if she woke him in the night, even if she was upset or frightened.

Ann recalled how she had driven past her exit on the highway yesterday, the second time she'd done that recently. The nightmare image of being locked in an empty house came back. She imagined just leaving everything and running away. Instead, she rolled onto her side to try to go back to sleep. "I'll be thirty-eight next month," she thought. "This is my lousy life."

The middle of the night is often a difficult time for the millions who are in unhappy marriages. They may be Ann's age, younger, or older. They may be men or women. They wake in a fitful state, and their thoughts go around and around with feelings of sadness and anger and fear, and wishes of what might have been or could be. They picture themselves with other partners, or compare their marriages and partners with others. They worry about their children, their finances, and how their lives are passing them by, with little hope of change. They ask themselves over and over: *Should I divorce? Do I have the courage? Can it ever get better? Will the children be okay if I get out? Will I be okay? Will I be alone forever? Can I afford to go? Can I endure if I do not? Do I stay in a deeply dissatisfying marriage? Is there any hope of change? Are the rare good times a sign that we still have something together? What do I face if I divorce?*

At one time or another, much of the adult married population has thought about these questions. Since 40 percent of the marriages in the United States end in divorce, many people spend a lot of time thinking about them. Many who cannot bring themselves to divorce are also plagued by these questions, but stoically persevere in desolate marriages. And many think about them, but ultimately decide the good outweighs the bad.

We do not advocate divorce, but, while a happy long-term marriage is certainly most desirable, this option is not always available or possible for many couples. At least 2.5 million American men and women—and more than 1 million children—live through divorce each year. We can safely assume that these people, as well as the millions in unhappy marriages who choose to stick it out, wrestle at length with the questions we raise.

Ten Steps to a Decision

The fears surrounding divorce are the same for almost everyone. This book provides ten steps to help you examine how serious the problems are in your marriage, what you might try to do to improve it, and, if that's not possible, considering whether it's time to separate and divorce. It presents the best research and personal examples about divorce drawn from twenty-five years of counseling individuals and couples, as well as scores of interviews conducted for the book. Whether you decide to stay and try to work it out, or go, this book will help you formulate a step-by-step, concrete plan for action.

Just as important as facing your fear of divorce is understanding the high cost of the alternative to divorce—continuing to live in an unhappy marriage. This book will provide you with guidance on what's important to make your marriage work better, and what steps to take to figure out if yours cannot.

Here is a summary of the steps we will discuss in detail throughout the book:

1. Determine: *Is my marriage unhappy? How unhappy am I?*
2. Ask yourself: *Is our parenting faltering?*
3. Look at your children right now: *Is our unhappy family affecting their school performance, behavior, and self-esteem?*
4. Face the truth: *What is the quality of our sexual life? Have we maintained emotional intimacy in our marriage?*
5. Assess: *Is marital stress affecting my physical and mental health? My children's? My spouse's?*

6. Take an inventory: *What are my fears about separating and divorcing? What stigma and shame do I fear from my family, friends, religion, and community?*
7. Evaluate your situation realistically: *If I divorce, what do I fear will happen to my children? Will I lose them? Can I accept not seeing them every day?*
8. Face your fears: *What financial repercussions of separation and divorce frighten me?*
9. Take another inventory: *Have I exhausted every remedy to heal my marriage? Do I have any realistic hope? What am I waiting for?*
10. Decide: *What is my plan?*

At the end of the discussion of each step, you'll find a summary of questions you need to ask yourself to help make a decision about how off track that aspect of your marriage may be. The questions are designed to hold up a mirror to your marriage, although the test itself is not a scientific evaluation. We recommend that you set a threshold for yourself. For most people, answering "yes" even 25 percent of the time signals that you may have serious problems in your marriage. If you answer "yes" to 50 percent or more of the questions, especially to the questions in step 9—*Have I exhausted every remedy?*—it's an even stronger signal that your marriage may be in serious trouble, and that you should seek professional help.

As you read this book, please keep the following statistics in mind:

- Five years after divorce at least 75 percent of women feel better off and have recovered financially, whether they initiated the divorce or not. Women initiate two-thirds of all separations, as reported by psychologist Judith Wallerstein in her book *Second Chances.*
- Also according to Wallerstein, after five years, two-thirds of men report strong preferences for their lives postdivorce.
- Two leading American professors of sociology, Frank Furstenburg and Andrew Cherlin, reported in their book *Divided Families* that two years after their parents' separation or divorce over two-thirds of the fifteen thousand children studied either stayed the same or improved in their schoolwork and behavior, compared with their performance prior to their parents' separation.

Part One

The Unhappy Marriage

CHAPTER 1

Defining the Unhappy Marriage

Step 1: Determine—Is my marriage unhappy? How unhappy am I?

Many people in unhappy marriages spend years convincing themselves that their marriage is no different than anyone else's. Their rationalizations include comforting statements like these: "Everyone argues sometimes," "It's normal for sex to become less interesting after a few years," "Most children talk back sometimes," "My parents' marriage was no picnic either," or "My mother told me that you shouldn't expect too much." So how do you know when you are not just comforting yourself, but kidding yourself instead? How do you know when you are making excuses and just marking time, or even wasting one precious year after another?

There are nine areas in a marriage in which couples must work out agreements with each other. In the 1980s, they were identified by family researchers James P. Peterson and Nicholas Zill and include:

- money, the most common source of discord in marriage
- parenting
- sex
- relationships with extended family and friends
- religion
- household responsibilities and gender roles
- substance use, including alcohol and drugs
- how to spend leisure time
- career and job-related issues

If you fail to create mutually acceptable understandings in three or more of the nine areas, your marriage is defined as "high conflict" or unhappy.

If you are in a marriage in which only one or two of the nine areas occasionally flare up, your marriage is considered to be healthy and relatively low conflict, even though arguments arise between you and your partner from time to time. In healthy marriages, most arguments are resolved often enough in a manner that both people can live with. If you fail to create mutually acceptable understandings in three or more of the nine areas, your marriage is defined as "high conflict" or unhappy.

A high-conflict marriage does not necessarily mean that you openly argue. For many couples, after some disagreement with no resolution, the conflicts are seldom or never discussed again. They go "underground," and are replaced by growing withdrawal, hidden anger, and silent or open disrespect.

In our interview with Lisa, she discussed her parents' marriage, and we saw two of the many areas of her parents' unresolved disagreements: their relations with extended family and their handling of money. Lisa related a recurring scene from her adolescence:

> A week didn't go by without my father tormenting my mother about how much he hated her younger sister, who was, in fact, nasty to my mother, but whom my mother loved nonetheless. It seemed to me that my mother got even with my father by belittling his ability to make money. My father was only home on Sundays, because he worked six days and nights. I always felt nervous as Sunday approached because they would usually argue and their arguments could really get out of hand, and I was afraid that somebody could get hurt. Maybe because I was a girl, I sympathized with my mother. I felt more and more distant from my father. I guess I grew up feeling men were the enemy. Although my parents are still together, I've been divorced twice.

Nothing Gets Resolved

Your marriage may not be as volatile as Lisa's parents'. Perhaps your disagreements wind up with one or the other of you just dropping out of the discussion, or saying, "Have it your way." The important question is—does anything the two of you disagree about ever really change? Are you in a marriage where you and your partner have disagreed about the same important issues year in and year out? When the two of you fall into one of your persistent disagreements, do you each feel stubbornly convinced of the rightness of your own point of view? Are you and your partner deaf to each other's perspectives?

Empathy and compassion break down. You may even start denying that your spouse has feelings. It may feel as if you are dealing with a stone.

Empathy Breaks Down

In an unhappy marriage, people are unable or unwilling to recognize the validity of the other person's position. You lose respect for one another, anger builds, and you pull away from each other. If this has been happening to you over and over, provoked by disagreements in a number of different areas, your marriage is not making you happy enough. We're not talking about happiness in some ideal sense. We are just saying "happy enough." This is the central question you are struggling with if you are reading this book: *Is my marriage happy enough?*

Steve told us that he dreaded opening the credit card bills every month. Just seeing them unopened in his stack of mail caused him to get a knot in his stomach. Steve had a good job, and he and his wife Ellen lived in a comfortable suburb with their two school-aged children. Over the fifteen years they had been married, they argued frequently about what he felt was Ellen's excessive spending. From Ellen's point of view, her expenditures were perfectly normal: clothes for their children, Jessie and Brian, new lamps for the family room, a new dress for herself for the holidays, visits to the vet for their dog, and food shopping. Steve would protest that she didn't have to go to the fanciest clothing store for clothes that the kids would soon outgrow. She didn't have to buy the most expensive cuts of beef in the supermarket, or spend hundreds of dollars on a dress for herself, or use any excuse to spend her days shopping in the mall. He repeatedly explained to her how much financial pressure he felt he was under; he encouraged her to get a job, all to no avail. Almost every month the credit card bills would be exorbitant, in Steve's opinion.

Ellen complained that he didn't respect her efforts to limit her spending. She also protested that she wanted their children to look as good as the neighbors' children, and that she wanted their house to look as good as their friends' homes. She felt that although he said he did, Steve didn't really place much importance on this. During several arguments, he threatened to take away Ellen's credit cards. She eventually went on a cash allowance instead, putting all her credit cards away, but typically wound up spending the cash Steve gave her only two weeks into the month. Then Steve had to give her more money. Eventually, she got her credit cards back.

So it continued: Steve would pay the bills, and he'd feel frustrated and angry with Ellen. Increasingly, he felt he was nothing more than a paycheck to her. These two people were completely lacking in the ability to come to terms about their finances, or understand one another's points of view, or feel any compassion for each other's needs. Eventually, they stopped fighting; in fact, they talked less and less about anything, their problems continued unresolved, and they grew more and more distant from one another.

Positions Harden

Steve and Ellen, like other couples in unhappy marriages, each hardened their positions. Ellen ignored Steve and shopped where she wanted to; Steve resented it. The danger in hardening your position is that it makes you deaf to your partner and makes you lose sight of any validity in his position. You stop seeing your partner as another adult, an "equal center of experience," as psychologist Jessica Benjamin has called each of us. Steve did not see Ellen as his wife and partner, but spoke of her as acting like a child. Ellen did not see Steve as a mature husband and wage earner, and a person of good judgment, but more as a tasteless cheapskate, who would embarrass the family in front of friends if he got his way.

Other Areas Break Down

The conflict over money spread to other areas of Steve and Ellen's marriage. Their sex life faltered because Ellen, who felt undermined by Steve, became increasingly unresponsive to him, and experienced his sexual desire as excessive. Steve confided his financial strains to his father. He naturally sided with Steve, and treated Ellen as if she were ruining his son financially. Steve offered no defense of Ellen to his father, but passively encouraged his father's anger toward his wife.

As Steve became convinced that he couldn't get Ellen to respond to any of his needs, or to respect him, he gradually started drinking to excess. He began flirting with other women, all of whom seemed much more responsive to him, respectful, and admiring. Ellen repeatedly criticized his increased drinking. He persisted, feeling that if she could ignore him, he could ignore her. Steve told us all of this a year after his separation, while he was in the process of getting divorced.

What's important to recognize from Steve and Ellen's story is the all-too-common progression in the unhappy marriage. It spirals downward. One or both of the partners is deaf to the other's perspective. They can't understand or relate to the feelings and motives of their spouse; they may even experience the other person as having no feelings at all. They keep a scorecard of wrongs, in which they increasingly feel victimized and self-righteous. Over time, they lose respect for the other person, whose point of view makes no sense to them, and who seems so absurdly stubborn. Alternatively, they feel hopeless because there is no way to appeal to the other's reason or emotion, and they believe the other will never yield, no matter what the cost.

Partners Stop Making an Effort

Some people respond to this breakdown by no longer making much effort to please their partner in daily life. It might be that a man comes home from work and repeatedly finds that his wife and kids are at her friend's house, with no dinner prepared, and no note or phone call. It could be that one or the other forgets to do or buy things that the other needs, or becomes more and more incapable of doing things correctly or competently. It may be that one or the other partner consistently forgets the other spouse's birthday, their wedding anniversary, or Valentine's Day.

Payback

Screwing up time after time on things your partner feels are important is often a sign of anger below the surface. Here are a few signs of suppressed anger that you may or may not even be aware of:

- Losing the house keys over and over
- Breaking glasses and dishes repeatedly
- Getting into fender benders repeatedly
- Persistently forgetting your obligations, like taking in the dry-cleaning or getting the car serviced
- Always giving your partner the car with an empty gas tank
- Forgetting to buy the food items your partner has repeatedly requested

Other people may resort to open or hidden forms of payback, such as speaking against the spouse to their children, friends, or relatives, or doing

Marriage counselors agree that when couples wait until their relationship is so deteriorated before they seek help, it's often too late.

things that they know will hurt or enrage the spouse. They may act out by withholding sex, flirting, or having an affair, or by being cruel or deliberately stubborn. These people consciously feel, "If you hurt me, I'll get even."

Even when it reaches these kinds of low points, what seems to keep people stuck in the purgatory of an unhappy marriage is the persistence of hope. You hope you will be able to find the right words or example that will persuade your mate, and get him or her to stop being deaf to you. Once attitudes are hardened, it is usually, although not always, futile to believe that you will bring about this change without a lot of motivation and professional help. The earlier you get this help, the better your chances for saving your marriage.

Deaf to Your Partner

Throughout their marriage, Esther criticized Ray for being unromantic and unaffectionate, and not taking an active enough role in their sex life. She also complained that Ray was passive in disciplining their children. In particular, she held Ray responsible for their son's poor grades in school. When Ray was disappointed that he didn't get a promotion he had thought was coming, Esther felt it was his own fault for not being aggressive enough with his boss. Esther felt this disappointment so keenly that she insisted they join a marriage encounter group at their church.

Ray went reluctantly. To put it in his words, he already "had a belly full" of criticism, and he only anticipated more of it in the group. He recalled that during the first couple of meetings, he said as little as possible and tried to keep a low profile. Esther, on the other hand, opened up to the group members and described her deep disappointments with Ray. To his surprise, other members of the group pointed out to Esther how unsympathetic she was toward Ray, and how critical she was of him. What shocked Ray even more was that Esther could not hear a single word of what they said to her. She was deaf to the group's unanimous feedback of how harsh she was to Ray. Nothing anyone said penetrated her self-righteousness and her feeling of being a victim. To this day, Ray looks back on those evenings in marriage encounter as the point when it started to dawn on him that he didn't have to keep thinking of himself in such a negative light. He saw how incapable

Esther was of seeing any of their problems as even partly her responsibility, and how hopeless that made their situation.

Balance of Power

Similarly, Carol has become completely deaf to Bill; in fact, she describes herself as "on strike." She refuses to do anything she doesn't want to do. She defies Bill, saying, "If you don't like it, divorce me." Bill doesn't want to do that, and she knows it. How did they get to this sorry state after eight years of marriage? Their story points out the important role the balance of power plays in marriage. From day 1, Bill decided everything—from how Carol should cut the vegetables, go shopping, and load the dishwasher, to how to raise their children, where to go on vacation, and what movie to see.

Every couple has to find their own balance of power. The cultural, religious, and family traditions with which you and your spouse were raised, as well as your own personalities, all figure prominently in the unique equation of shared power and control in your marriage. Some people have a high tolerance for large imbalances of power and decision making in their marriage, others do not; each of us creates our own rules for keeping score. Each of us knows when we have reached a point that no longer seems fair. We may have swept power imbalances under the rug for a long time, but eventually we begin to trip over them. Power imbalance in marriage is a serious problem. Researchers at the University of Pennsylvania Medical School found a significantly higher risk of death among older women in a fifteen-year study of the effects of unequal decision-making power in marriage. The same does not hold true for men because the imbalance of power almost always favors the man.

A well-known researcher on marital relationships, John Gottman, in his book *Why Marriages Succeed or Fail,* states that "When a man or woman is not willing to share power with his partner, there is a great chance that the marriage will eventually self-destruct." This seems to reflect what is happening to Bill and Carol. Carol is tripping over the power imbalance that has been swept under the carpet in her marriage for many years.

Bill was raised in a family that fostered little respect for women. He is five years older than Carol, and they married when she was quite young. She saw Bill as more worldly and experienced than she was. She thought that if she accommodated his needs and fell in line with his decisions, he would grow to admire and respect her. Exactly the opposite occurred. Her

Often, in an unhappy marriage, one or both partners continues to mature, but the relationship does not.

compliance and ceding of power in the relationship to Bill just emboldened him; in fact, it made Bill act increasingly condescending toward her. But now, eight years into their marriage Carol is in her early thirties. She is a mother, she has a responsible job where her work is valued, and she is respected. Carol gets enough confirmation from the world outside her marriage to know that there is something radically wrong with her relationship inside her marriage.

In addition to a lack of balance of power, Carol and Bill's story points out one of the most common failures in unhappy marriages—one or both partners continues to mature, but the relationship does not. The marriage remains stuck in the past, more like the younger, less mature relationship they formed when they first got together. A couple we interviewed whose marriage we admire told us that in their forty years together they feel that they have had seven different marriages. Each of these "marriages" symbolized an impasse they had reached and overcome together before they could move on. Each "marriage" represented a different stage of maturity in their lives and a new rebalancing of power between them.

As Carol has become more confrontational with Bill, he has registered shock that she is so unhappy. He even says he feels contrite. He blames himself for being a "control freak." He says he loves Carol and wants to keep their family together, that he didn't realize she was keeping score. Carol feels that she's at the brink. What should she do? We believe Carol and Bill haven't exhausted every remedy. We believe she should take Bill at his word. With professional help, they may be able to readjust the balance of power in their marriage in a way that would enable each of them to feel heard, and which might allow greater closeness and mutual respect to grow between them.

Just a Rough Patch

Thinking about the problems in a marriage provokes powerful feelings of guilt and self-doubt in each of us. *Am I just selfish? Am I being unrealistic about what marriage is supposed to be? Do I want too much out of life? Why can't I just be content with all the good things I have in my life? My partner probably isn't that bad; I'm just overreacting. It's all my fault. I chose him [or her]; I knew what I was getting myself into. I wish he [or she] would do something really awful; then it would be easy for me to make up my mind.*

Part of the self-doubt may be fueled by the years of your mate tearing you down. We lose confidence in ourselves in a bad marriage.

We may stay on this internal treadmill for years, alternating between feelings of anger, guilt, and despair. With each day that provides fresh evidence of how awful our mate is, the next one finds us cringing and full of self-recrimination for feeling that way and blaming ourselves for our marriage's failures. Sometimes this alternates with feeling more hopeful because we share a good evening, weekend, or even a vacation. How do you know if the hard times are just a phase your marriage is going through, something that the two of you can work out if you can get past this rough patch? How do you know if, years from now, you may be able to look back and feel grateful that you stuck it out and saw it through? One way to know is to ask yourself how much you two love each other, and how motivated you both are to get things back on track.

For some couples, the key to getting past a rough patch lies in how willingly and frequently they can express how much they love each other, and how wholeheartedly they both feel they are willing to do whatever it takes to turn their problems around.

Greg and Melinda's marriage had been happy until the birth of their first child. She stopped working, reducing their income, and he started working harder in his pharmacy business to offset the lost wages. She found motherhood very stressful. He worked late, came home exhausted, but Melinda, stressed by a long day with the baby, would hand the baby off to him the second he walked through the door. This made him resentful. So Greg started working longer and longer hours, six days a week. Even on his day off, he avoided doing child care whenever he could get away with it. When he was around, however, he made many recommendations on how to manage the baby, which Melinda resented enormously. The baby wasn't the easiest infant. He cried because he was a little colicky. Greg and Melinda grew wary of each other. She felt "stuck with the baby," and he felt she was almost always in a bad mood. He felt Melinda gave everything to the baby and almost nothing to him. In particular, he resented her for not getting out of her bathrobe during the day or straightening the house, and most especially, he resented her lost interest in having sex.

Their "rough patch" lasted a couple of years. The turning point came in the midst of a terrible argument when Melinda blurted out to Greg that maybe he should move out. Both were shocked by this. They started talking to each other about how much they loved each other, and how frightened they were that they had gotten to this terrible place. They both felt that they should go into counseling. Very rapidly, Greg agreed to hire a part-time assistant for his business in order to free up some of his time, and they hired a babysitter a couple of days a week so Melinda could have some time for herself. This caused some financial hardship, but they both felt it was important, so they used part of their savings and deferred contributing money to their retirement account. They instituted dates with one another, without the baby, and they started trying to listen to each other when either one was distressed. Melinda and Greg were fortunate. They both wanted the same thing.

Signs of Alienation

Alternatively, how do you know if years from now you will look back and say, "Why did I waste so many years? The signs were so clear that my mate refused to try and my marriage was over. How could I not have paid attention to them?" How do you know if it's time to go? One measure is how alienated you two are from each other.

Agnes told us that when Charles bought a small motorboat without even mentioning this purchase to her in advance, she was shocked. She hadn't even known a boat was something Charles wanted. They talked so little, except when they fought with one another. Worse still, after he told her, and before he took delivery of the boat, Agnes began to imagine what it would be like spending Sundays alone with Charles in the middle of the water, with no friends or relatives around and no place to go to avoid Charles. Agnes recounted:

> I realized I was in terrible trouble when Charles bought the boat. It was suddenly so clear that I was staying in my marriage because I had figured out how to spend almost no time alone with my husband. When I was with Charles, I felt so much lonelier than when I was either alone or with anyone else on the planet. That was the realization that helped me to make the decision to separate from Charles. I never did go on that boat with him.

Randy, who had been married to Kate for nine years, told us that night after night he would get into bed and watch the 11 o'clock news while Kate sat working at the kitchen table. He would often ask her to get into bed with him, but she would decline, saying, "I just have too much work" or "I'm just more ambitious than you are. I want to make something of myself." Over and over again, Randy would fall asleep with the television on, feeling rejected, angry, old, and lonely at forty, and wondering if anything would ever happen that could make that change. This couple's alienation also led to avoidance of one another, both in and out of their bedroom.

Of course, we don't know Charles's or Kate's sides of these stories, but we can imagine some of their frustration. We know Charles has to have felt pretty alienated from Agnes if he never shared his dream of buying a boat with her, and, even worse, that he made such a substantial investment and commitment without first discussing it with his wife. When Kate declined Randy's frequent requests to come to bed with him with a retort expressing how superior she felt, she was also probably feeling, "You don't take care of my needs, so why should I take care of yours?"

Shifting Intimacy

Randy told us that after years of Kate's avoiding him he started developing an office friendship with Suzanne, a married woman with whom he had worked for a long time. Suzanne had just been a casual friend, like any other colleague. One day while making small talk, Randy realized how much he was enjoying Suzanne's company, and that she seemed to be enjoying his. Suzanne's interest, admiration, and warmth were a breath of fresh air. Randy began to look for excuses to have these friendly chats. Gradually, their conversations extended to sometimes going out to lunch together. Over time, they shared confidences about the difficulties and unhappiness that each of them experienced in their marriages. Randy found Suzanne very attractive, although he never allowed himself to act on it, and he never spoke to Suzanne about it. He felt critical of himself that these thoughts came to mind. What he didn't recognize was that close emotional connections, where intimate details of a marriage are revealed to another person, drain the emotional life of a marriage even further. Sex doesn't have to figure into it at all.

In the same way, Agnes observed that during the years she was married to Charles, her friendship with Lynn, her oldest and dearest friend, became closer as the distance between Agnes and Charles grew. Lynn also was unhappy with her marriage and the two women treasured the mutual solace they found talking about their marital disappointments and dissatisfactions. Charles was

When someone else—a sister or brother, a coworker, or friend—becomes more emotionally intimate with you than your spouse is, your marriage is off track.

somewhat aware of this. He complained to Agnes that he felt excluded and that her loyalties were greater to Lynn than to him. He wasn't wrong.

Shifting Loyalty

The marriage ceremony represents a shifting of loyalties from your parents or friends to your partner, and the creation of your new family.

Many people don't make this shift when they get married. They have already developed their closest intimate relationship with a brother, sister, parent, or friend. In this closest relationship, they feel truly safe talking about anything; they feel totally accepted. If this sounds like you or your mate, your marriage may not have gotten off to the best start. It is already being deprived of some of the closeness that it needs.

Long ago, it was a custom in Japan that, when a young woman married, she would leave her parents' home to go to the wedding ceremony. As she walked down the path away from the house, her mother would follow her with a broom to sweep the bride's footsteps away. This is a powerful symbolic gesture, and a wise one. The bride may never return to her parents' home on the same path. Her allegiance is now to her new family. The new path is the one she and her husband are about to set off on. They will create their own home and their own family.

If the husband's or wife's loyalty or emotional intimacy shifts to another person, away from the spouse, it is a sign of a problem in a marriage. Well-known family therapist Eleanor Craig-Green says, "There already has to be a big space between a husband and wife before someone else can move in to fill it." It almost doesn't matter whether it is a member of the opposite sex or the same sex.

Both men and women have confided to us in interviews that they have an opposite-sex friend at work with whom they can speak more openly and closely than they can with their spouse. They usually do not see this as problematic for their marriage. It is. Their intimate conversations with these office mates or friends usually reflect the conversations they are not having with their spouses. When asked about this, they often say that their spouse isn't interested or is too tired and preoccupied, and that the friend is genuinely interested. If this is happening to you, it probably means that too many of the nine areas that couples need to agree on remain unresolved between you and your partner.

Revisiting the Nine Areas

So it's essential for a couple to establish a mutually acceptable understanding in at least seven or eight of the nine areas to enjoy the good communication that is crucial to a reasonably happy marriage. Once again, they are:

- money, the most common source of discord in marriage
- parenting
- sex
- relationships with extended family and friends
- religion
- household responsibilities and gender roles
- substance use, including alcohol and drugs
- how to spend leisure time
- career and job-related issues

In the areas where a couple is unable to come to a mutually acceptable agreement, they nonetheless need to find a way to address and work with each other, or at least work around the issues in those areas.

For example, Lisa's father and mother could not agree on the kind of relationship they should have with her mom's younger sister. Lisa's dad wanted absolutely no contact whatsoever with his sister-in-law. Lisa's mom wanted a close daily relationship. Instead of a constant impasse that continually exacerbated their differences, this couple needed to find a reasonable accommodation together. The sister might have been able to visit when the husband wasn't home, or the wife might have visited at the sister's home. Perhaps they needed a second telephone so the wife could call the sister whenever she wanted without tying up the family line and creating the occasion for yet another angry outburst.

When too many disagreements remain unresolved; if there is complete inflexibility on your mate's part, or things consistently don't go your way; if it's always up to you to make the adjustment, alienation and disrespect grow. This is likely to create further disagreements in other areas. Each of you hardens your position, even if you superficially go along to avoid making things worse. You become deaf to your partner's point of view. You experience your spouse as being inflexible, unyielding, and unfeeling. You lose empathy and compassion and pull further away. You may be inclined to confide in someone else, someone whom you feel understands you better than your mate, someone who accepts you and hears you. If you see yourself in the examples we provide, these are signs that you may be unhappy and that your marriage may also be suffering. They are not necessarily signs that it is time to go, but it is time to take definitive action to see if you can get your marriage back on track. One step may be to tell your spouse you are reading this book, and suggest that he read it, too.

Questions to Think About

1. Do my spouse and I disagree on at least three of the nine areas (see page 3) in which all couples must work out agreements? Yes___No___

2. Have our persistent disagreements led to open or hidden anger and disrespect between us? Yes___No___

3. For the most part, have my spouse and I stopped trying to please each other in the areas that really matter to each of us? Yes___No___

4. Do I feel that the scorecard of "rights and wrongs" between us is strongly out of balance? Yes___No___

5. Is there too great an imbalance of power between us in the relationship? Yes___No___

6. Are we stuck in habits we formed when we were much less mature people? Yes___No___

7. Do we avoid spending time together? Yes___No___

8. Do I feel more accepted and respected by a family member, a same-sex friend, or a colleague than I do by my spouse? Yes___No___

CHAPTER 2

The Marriage Bill of Rights

We recently read an article titled "Defending the Comatose Marriage." The authors, psychologists who are "marital experts," write in Men.Style.Com, a lifestyle blog for men, about what they call "zombie marriages." They write: "No matter how many stakes are driven through its heart, it will continue to stumble forward . . . No matter how strong a union is when it's formed, inevitably it begins to take on an almost [zombie-like] quality . . . People just get in a routine. They go on automatic." The authors refer to this as "settling in."

That sounds to us like settling for far too little. You can't let your mate use excuses like the demands of children, or work, or both as a complete cop-out in your marriage. You have the right to expect some things from your marriage that you cannot get, or should not seek, outside of it. We propose that you measure your marriage against our Marriage Bill of Rights. We believe that if your marriage is failing in even one or two of the areas listed in this chapter, you have serious problems. If your marriage is failing in four or more of the ten areas, you may even have irreparable marital problems.

The Marriage Bill of Rights

1. You have a right to expect *loyalty* from your mate. Your partner should not put loyalty to family or friends ahead of his loyalty to you, just as you can't expect a neighbor or friend to put loyalty to you before loyalty to his own partner and family. You need to get loyalty from your mate.
2. You have a right to expect your mate to be your *protector,* to serve as a buffer between you and the difficulties of life. Who else is there to do this for you if not your mate? If you're still

relying on your parents to protect you from life's hardships and vicissitudes, you are forced into remaining in a childlike role.

3. You have a right to expect *affection* from your mate. Everyone needs some degree of affection. If you don't get it from your mate, where should it come from?
4. You have a right to expect your mate to be your *partner* in the tasks of life. Even though your workloads and commitments may be very different, marriage is a partnership with some hopefully compassionate and enlightened division of labor.
5. You have a right to expect your mate to be your *caregiver* when you need care. Why did you form a family if you cannot depend on one another in a time of need? We don't only mean when you are sick or at death's door; we mean responding to the small needs each of us has every day.
6. You have a right to a mate who is *supportive,* who is on your team, who is not overly critical, and from whom you get at least an occasional pat on the back for who you are as a person. She chose you. You aren't a commodity or a toy or a checkbook, to be tossed in the back of the closet because of boredom, or to be taken for granted.
7. You have a right to expect some *companionship* from your mate. He doesn't have to be joined at the hip with you, but presumably you came together because you enjoyed each other's company. You have more in common now, whether you realize it or not, and are more familiar and ought to be more comfortable with one another than ever. If that's not the basis for true companionship, something is radically wrong between you.
8. You have a right to live in a marriage that affords you some degree of *freedom*. Life, liberty, and the pursuit of happiness apply to marriage as well as citizenship. You should be able to pursue activities and the company of other people that provide you with opportunities for personal maturity and growth, achievement, and social companionship. Men—and it is mostly men—sometimes exert unreasonably controlling restrictions on their wives' most basic freedom of action. We have heard story after story of men who control their wives' friendships, family contacts, opportunities to work or

take classes—even to drive a car, have any access to money, and, in the extreme, to leave the house. We consider this a violation of basic human rights as well as of the marriage bill of rights.

9. You have a right to expect *honest* communication from your spouse, to the limit of her ability to be honest with herself. It isn't acceptable for your partner to hold deep, dark secrets about issues that bear on both of your lives. If your mate has a health issue, a financial issue, an issue of fidelity, drug or alcohol abuse, or any other issue that seriously impacts each of you, it's her obligation to consult with you about it. Marriage is a partnership.
10. You have a right to be treated with *respect*. Your partner should grant you the same courtesy and respect that he gives to colleagues at work, to respected family members, or to your religious leaders. If anything, you should get more respect. If you don't demand respect, don't be surprised that you are not getting it. Plato wisely said, "We get the behavior from other people that we accept."

No, a "zombie marriage" is unacceptable. Too many stakes through the heart and your marriage is dead. Get real about the Marriage Bill of Rights. If your mate doesn't match up to every one of them, there is room for growth and forgiveness. But if he or she matches up in only a few areas or none, your marriage doesn't meet even the most modest expectations. Things must change or you should consider if it's time to go.

Questions to Think About

1. Do I feel that my mate is not sufficiently loyal to me? Yes___No___
2. Do I feel that my mate is not sufficiently protective of me? Yes___No___
3. Do I feel that my marriage lacks affection? Yes___No___
4. Is there an unfair division of labor in my marriage? Yes___No___

5. Has my mate let me down when I needed physical or emotional caring? Yes___No___
6. Do I feel taken for granted in my marriage? Yes___No___
7. Do I lack sufficient companionship in my marriage? Yes___No___

CHAPTER 3

How Parenting Falters

Step 2: Ask yourself—Is our parenting faltering?

We met Don, Alice, and their son Jake when Jake was thirteen years old. Alice is more the disciplinarian and Don is the more indulgent and permissive parent. Alice and Don disagree about this often, and many other things as well.

Don is a successful businessman and Alice is a stay-at-home mom. Despite Don's business success, he can be passive in the marriage and in the family. Alice makes most of the family decisions, even if Don disagrees. She has often acted unilaterally, with no consultation, and if Don protested, she might ignore him or become verbally abusive in front of Jake and his little brother Martin. Don, for his part, describes himself as "staying above it all." The louder Alice gets, the quieter Don becomes.

Don acts dismissively toward Alice. He talks about her to Jake behind her back, telling him that his mother is "overemotional." In front of the children, Don often undermines Alice. He rolls his eyes in disrespect of Alice when she takes what she feels is a firm stand, and he openly labels most of her attempts to discipline Jake as "overreaction."

Don believes he is forming a strong alliance with Jake. Despite the fact that he appears to side with his father, Jake is caught on the horns of a dilemma. How can he accept guidance from either of his parents? If he sides with his mother, he is betraying his father. If he sides with his father, he is betraying his mother. As a result, Jake seems to have adopted an "I don't care policy." He has shut out both his parents, and rejects almost everything they say. He no longer seems to care about the consequences of his behavior. Many people would say this is typical of a teenager. It isn't. Jake is very distressed by what's going on between his parents, and he doesn't know which way to turn.

In unhappy marriages, parenting may become polarized. One parent feels the other is too harsh with the children. He or she counterbalances the perceived harshness with leniency. The more the strict parent behaves strictly, the more the lenient parent behaves leniently, exacerbating the situation.

Recently, Jake was caught cheating on a test in school by his teacher. The teacher contacted his parents. This was serious; just weeks before he had been suspended for cutting classes. Alice was outraged at Jake. She wanted to ground him for a month. Don wanted to make light of it. He told Jake his behavior was wrong, but that his mother was overreacting, as usual. Alice was adamant. Don gave in to her, but only on the surface. He undermined Alice by letting Jake go out to study with a schoolmate, when the boy was supposed to be home studying.

Polarized Parents

Parenting often falters in families where there is a parent-versus-parent struggle. It's not unusual for children in these families to become pawns in the struggle. If children side with one parent, they feel as if they are betraying the other parent.

In this chapter, we focus on some of the more common ways in which parenting falters in the unhappy marriage. While it's impossible to completely separate this parenting from the impact it has on children, in the next chapter we concentrate on how children respond.

In Don and Alice's marriage, consistency in child rearing is obviously failing. Jake is a pawn in his parents' power struggle. Neither Don nor Alice is right, and neither is an effective parent. Neither is willing to collaborate with or support the other when it comes to decisions regarding their children. Each parent is determined to win the "which parent will prevail game." Increasingly, Jake is running into more severe problems. Last term he failed two courses.

Unhappy marriages promote anger, depression, and despair in the partners. That's why it's no surprise that parenting tends to get off track in the unhappy family. Parenting in these families can be unaffectionate and neglectful, or overly affectionate and smothering. It can set too many and too rigid limits on children's behavior, or too few and inconsistent limits. Children of unhappy marriages often don't receive the nurturance and guidance they require. Parents' energies are diverted by their irreconcilable differences. Frequently, parents become self-absorbed and may become overly preoccupied with activities and relationships outside the family, and neglectful of the children.

Each of his parents blames Jake's behavior on the other parent. Don and Alice briefly sought marital counseling to see if they could act cooperatively to help Jake. After a few sessions, Alice refused to continue when it became apparent that she'd have to accept some of the responsibility for this crisis with their son.

When there is a power struggle going on between parents, there is pressure for the child to take sides. Because he is male, and because his dad is the more lenient parent, Jake is more estranged from his mom than his dad. This seriously inhibits his relationship with his mother and prevents them from developing normal closeness and intimacy. Jake is learning to feel disrespectful toward women, and this may affect his relationships with women for the rest of his life, including, someday, in his own marriage. We've seen the results of this pattern in several adult men who grew up in similar circumstances and who have lived through multiple divorces.

Competitive Parents

Like Jake, Robin became a pawn in the power struggle between her parents. For years, Joan and Javier were in a toxic relationship in which each was endlessly competitive with the other. Foolishly, they hoped that having a child might bring them closer together. Many couples have tried this, and it almost invariably backfires. Anyone who has had a child knows that raising a baby is stressful, expensive, and very time-consuming. It puts all kinds of additional stresses on even a good marriage.

Javier told us that from the time their daughter Robin was less than one year old, when she and Javier were playing together and having a good time, his wife Joan would routinely insert herself into the activity to get Robin's attention away from Javier and to focus on her. Javier complained about this to Joan. He wanted her to see that when she played with Robin, he didn't try to come between them. Joan claimed that she had no idea what he was talking about and that he was being paranoid, as usual. She said he was jealous of the closer relationship she was forming with their little daughter.

As Robin grew older, she seemed increasingly uneasy playing with Javier if her mom was around. By the time she was about five, whenever

Robin and Javier spent time together, Robin wanted to include her mom. She would say she didn't want her mom to feel left out, or hurt her mom's feelings. It seems that Robin started feeling guilty when she felt close to, or was enjoying time with her father, and that she was betraying her mother if she didn't include her when she played with her dad. Javier also told us that even if Joan was at work or out shopping, and he and Robin were alone, she would consistently make mention of her mom, saying things like "Mom and I did this yesterday" or "Mom and I had more fun when we went to the park."

Perhaps without realizing it, Joan appears to have created a sense that "Three's a crowd," instead of welcoming her husband's love and involvement with their daughter. This parental power struggle was just one symptom of the deep marital problems that eventually led to Joan and Javier's divorce.

Smothering Parents

Another way that parenting falters in the unhappy family involves a parent becoming too dependent on a child to make up for the lack of closeness with his or her spouse. These parents may become overly protective and possessive of their children. The child may also become too dependent on the parent and have great difficulty moving toward independence in adulthood.

Lena, a woman in her early thirties, described her parents to us. Her mom was lonely. Her dad not only worked very long hours, but virtually never came home until late at night because of his involvement with several volunteer organizations, and a regular weekly card game. There was almost no married life or family life, and when her dad was home, her parents often argued bitterly. Lena, an only child, became the focus of her mother's love and attention. They ate meals together, saw movies and watched TV together, and visited neighbors and relatives together. As a little girl, Lena promised that when she got married someday they would all live in a two-family house together. At night Lena would lie in bed with her mother before going to sleep, and often, the two of them would laugh hysterically, making fun of Lena's dad and his many outside pursuits.

As Lena grew older and children her age were going to sleepaway camp, Lena's mother feared that Lena was "such a pretty child she'd be easy prey for older boys." She refused to let Lena go to camp and impressed upon her that she should be frightened of the "dangers out there waiting for her." Lena gradually accepted this notion about herself and became progressively more fearful. She actually became too frightened to stay away from home, even for supervised sleepovers at the homes of other children, which all the other girls relished attending.

In the absence of a reasonably fulfiling marriage, some parents develop an overdependence on a child to make up for the emotional, and perhaps physical, absence of the spouse.

This worked out conveniently for both of her parents. Her father could stay out night after night without feeling guilty about leaving his wife all alone. Lena's mother had a built-in companion, one who had little interest in separating from her mother to spend more time with her peers. The mother enforced rigid and excessive limits on what Lena could and could not do. All through Lena's adolescence, her mother continued to emphasize dangers in the outside world. Girlfriends Lena chose were "bad influences" and any boys who showed an interest in Lena "just wanted sex." This became the rationale for Lena's mother convincing her not to go away to college.

In this type of situation, the parent treats the child as if she were fearful or vulnerable. What the parent fails to see is that her own loneliness is prompting her excessive involvement with her child. Like Lena, the child usually falls in line with the parent's point of view.

There is real sadness listening to the stories told by adult children who grew up in unhappy families. Part of it stems from the memories they cling to in order to persuade themselves that their family was "normal" and "like other families." Lena recalled:

> No matter how much my parents argued and avoided each other, I also remember the good times when my dad was around and we were all together. My father had an old car, a Dodge, with poor suspension. I remember laughing our heads off riding down bumpy roads in that car. Sometimes we would all play Monopoly together. My father loved to win. Mom and I didn't really care. Some Sundays we would go out for Chinese food; I hated Chinese food, but I loved the idea of our little family being together. Still, ours was never a real home. I envied other kids and their families. Their homes seemed safer and more welcoming.

As people recount their sad stories of neglect, and even of cruel abuse in their unhappy families, they often describe their families and parents as "normal," sometimes even as "happy." Lena told us that her father would laughingly dub his family philosophy "wholesome neglect." She told us that when she was a child, she believed this must be a good thing.

The majority of adults in unhappy marriages and families cling to the relatively few happy times like a life preserver, so they don't have to face the consequences of seeing their situations clearly. If you face your situation, you may feel compelled to make it better or end it.

No Sense of Home

While her family lived in three different places during her childhood and adolescence, that wasn't, according to Lena, what kept it from feeling like home. Her mother, who seems to have suffered from depression, had no interest in anything domestic. The house was always a mess; laundry wouldn't get done, sometimes for months; meals were erratic; menus were whatever happened to be in the refrigerator. This neglect was one of the reasons why Lena's father stayed away so many nights, and also one of the sources of bitterness between her parents on the nights when her dad did show up. Neither Lena nor her father felt that the family home was a welcoming enough place. Nonetheless, Lena and her mother formed a powerful alliance.

Good parenting includes creating a "home." We asked people we interviewed what *home* means to them. They told us that feeling a sense of "home" encompasses feeling "safe," "nurtured," "loved," "guided," "sponsored," and "valued and accepted for who you are." Home is truly where the heart is.

Lena told us that at twenty she married a young man who was a very poor choice for her: "In hindsight I married to get away from my lonely, depressed, and controlling mother, and my mostly absent, usually angry father. I just wouldn't be my mother's slave for the rest of my life." Lena's marriage only lasted a couple of years.

When there is tension and conflict between a husband and wife, a few likely scenarios affect parenting. One scenario is that both parents use the children as pawns to act out a power struggle between them. In this case, the needs of the children matter less than which of the parents feels they are prevailing in their influence over the children. This seems to be the case with

Jake and Robin, and their parents. A second scenario is one in which one or both parents become overly involved with the child, using the child, as Lena was used, to satisfy adult needs that the parents' marriage should be fulfilling.

Too often an acceptable way of "dropping out" of family life is by spending excessive time on a career. Being a great provider is not a synonym for being a great parent or mate.

Dropping Out

Parenting may also falter in an unhappy marriage when one or both partners essentially drop out of the marriage and family, replacing family life with their own pursuits and objectives. They no longer have most of their needs met in the family. If this applies to both parents, children are left too much on their own without guidance or nurturance. These are neglectful parents.

Structure, which children need daily, may be absent or erratic, and children's inappropriate behaviors may be ignored. Sometimes one or both parents become so preoccupied, self-absorbed, and stressed that they fail to censor their own inappropriate behaviors. They don't shield their children from witnessing their own angry outbursts, extreme disrespect, or excessive drug or alcohol use.

We have too many stories to recount all of the shocking neglect we heard from people we interviewed who grew up in unhappy families: the four-year-old whose mother and father would sometimes lock her in the apartment all day and leave for work; the little boy who got impetigo, a disease known almost exclusively in the poorest parts of the developing world, because his mother left him so filthy; the girl who reported that her school insisted that her mother take a course on nutrition because she and her brother exhibited signs of malnutrition. These children had a few things in common: They came from middle-class homes with educated parents, and their parents were so unhappily married, and consumed by anger and depression, that they had little to give to their children and were unable to fulfill the most basic responsibilities of parenthood. We have recounted some of the more shocking examples of neglect we've come upon. Much more common, but still very damaging, are the parents who are excessively self-preoccupied and resort to overuse of electronic babysitters—television, video games and computers—or rely excessively on paid babysitters or nannies. You need to give careful thought to whether any of these examples apply to you. Too often an acceptable way of "dropping out" of family life is by spending excessive time on a career. Being a great provider is not a synonym for being a great parent or mate.

Not Owning Problems

The Kabbalah, a mystical Jewish text, talks about "those who are lost" and "those who are twice lost." The "lost" are unhappy and they know it; they cannot find their way out of their suffering. Their lives are robbed of meaning and comfort. But the Kabbalah says there is hope for them if they keep struggling to solve their problems. The "twice lost" are those who are lost and do not know it. Many of the parents we are describing are among the twice lost. They fail to recognize or acknowledge the pain that they live with or create, so they don't do anything about it.

Crystal, a forty-year-old woman, came to therapy to talk about her workaholism. She suffered from fatigue and anxiety; she felt it was the result of her perfectionism and excessive ambition. She was, by any measure, a very successful businesswoman. She traveled weekly on business, worked at home on weekends, and had little time for her daughter or her second husband. Her goal in therapy was to get her work anxiety under control because it was draining her energy unnecessarily. She had no interest in talking about her relationships with her daughter or her husband. "They're fine," she'd affirm. Crystal was twice lost. Actually, her business was the part of her life that was working best. She was avoiding the relationships with both her daughter and her husband, and not putting the energy that was needed into either of them.

On the surface Crystal's husband, Gil, was a good husband. He wasn't cruel or unfaithful. He was reasonably hardworking and social, and a great dancer and dresser. When Crystal eventually started talking about him in her therapy, what surfaced was that her relationship with Gil was passive and empty. They didn't fight, but they didn't connect, either. Crystal reported that her husband barely noticed when she went away on business. He didn't protest her obsession with her work. He was withdrawn from any real intimacy with Crystal or genuine closeness with his stepdaughter, although he acted responsibly as the adult in the house when Crystal was away.

As Crystal talked more about Gil, it became clear that he was an angry, withholding, unbending, and passionless man, who saw Crystal and her daughter as a burden. He was absorbed by self-criticism and personal disappointment. It became clear that Crystal's workaholism and lack of fulfillment in her marriage were different sides of the same coin. The emptier things became in her marriage, the harder she worked, and the more she traveled in order to build her business. Work was where she felt the greatest control and satisfaction.

Her small daughter, Heather, was an only child and, as all children do, needed lots of attention. Unfortunately, Heather couldn't compete with Crystal's business in fulfilling her mom's ambition. Crystal focused on her business night and day, and Heather was mostly left to her passive stepfather, who was absent in his own way. For almost seven years, beginning when Heather was around eight years old, Crystal neglected many of Heather's needs for an involved mother, an intimate parental relationship, and a "home." Crystal said that Heather once told her that during some of those years she liked to sit on the floor of her mother's closet for an hour or more at a time, taking in her absent mom's scent and trying to be closer to her when Mom was away on a business trip.

Even when she wasn't traveling on business, Crystal felt that she really didn't have time to shop and cook, and that Gil "couldn't boil water without burning it" so the refrigerator in their home was empty most of the time. Many nights when she was home, Crystal would send Heather down to the local store to buy take-out dinners for the family. They would talk, but without much real connection. Crystal would often lie in bed, chastising herself for being so anxious so much of the time, vaguely realizing that she must be communicating this to Heather. When she wasn't traveling, Crystal spent many evenings going out with Gil to cultivate more business contacts, further decreasing her availability to Heather.

Crystal was very lucky: Heather was a well-behaved girl and a good student, and although she was more or less forced to raise herself, kept to a straight path. Oftentimes, the mother and daughter's main subjects of communication became how well things were going for Crystal in her business and what problems Heather was having, especially socially or physically. It seemed as if the best way Heather could get Crystal's attention was if something was wrong in her life, or if she didn't feel well. Heather gradually withdrew from Crystal, and shut her out in many ways. Crystal's neglect of Heather didn't show up significantly until Heather started dating.

Then Heather would typically become attracted to boys who were distant and self-absorbed, in some ways like her mother, and eventually Heather would feel hurt and rejected by them.

Eventually, by facing the realities of her marriage, her neglect of her daughter, and her reasons for taking so much refuge in her business, Crystal was able to break her pattern of being "twice lost." She began to show much greater motivation to spend time with Heather, and to face whether her marriage was viable. In time, she decided it was not, and she divorced Gil. Now Crystal has built a relationship with her daughter that is one of the great satisfactions of her life.

Unpredictable Parenting

Another way that parenting falters in the unhappy marriage is when parents fail to act with any predictability in dealing with their children: sometimes loving, sometimes cold, sometimes strict, sometimes neglectful. The children in these families grow up never quite knowing what to expect from their parents. Alan's family was like this. He observed that his parents rarely showed each other any affection. They argued about him and his brother, about the in-laws on both sides of the family, and about one another's real or imagined flirtations outside the marriage, which aroused intense jealousy in the other. They also argued frequently about not having enough money. Alan recalled that one minute they seemed relatively happy, the next they would be arguing loudly. Alan would try to make peace between them, sometimes physically inserting himself between them if they threatened to become violent toward one another.

Alan told us that when he was in grade school, sometimes his mom would insist that he stay home after school to do his homework, and she would work with him and check it carefully. Other times she didn't seem to care at all. For weeks he would barely do his homework and stay out playing with his friends. His mom seemed to accept this, then, unpredictably she would fly into a rage and scream at Alan for not doing his assignments. Alan's father could be equally inconsistent. Sometimes he was gentle and involved, taking his son on nature walks, carefully explaining the fascinating aspects of what they observed. But often his father would lose his temper, criticize Alan, call him names, or be physically abusive to him. At times Alan's mother would rush to protect and defend him; other times she would not. He never knew what was expected of him or what to expect. Sometimes she would praise Alan exaggeratedly and draw him very close to her. At other times, she would ignore him totally. In hindsight, Alan feels his parents' behavior toward him mirrored how they were feeling toward each other at any given moment.

In unhappy families, many children come to believe that they are to blame for their parents' arguing and unhappiness, and that they are unlovable or bad children because their parents fight about them so much.

As an adolescent, Alan's behavior was equally volatile and unpredictable. Usually he was well-behaved, even timid. At other times he could be a bully and act like a delinquent. He hung out with tough kids, got into fights, and even had some trouble with the authorities. Sometimes in school he would get A's; other times he received F's. There was no consistency in Alan's home, or in Alan himself. He remembers wondering if his parents loved each other. They said they did, but their behavior usually indicated just the opposite. He didn't know if they loved or hated him; sometimes they acted one way, sometimes the other.

Alan eventually decided that both of his parents were crazy and he told them so in typical inept adolescent ways. His outbursts would unite his parents temporarily. They would turn on him and accuse him of being the crazy one. As Jake has done with his parents, Alan gradually learned to disregard them. He no longer took any guidance from, felt trust in, or believed either of his parents. Yet they remained unable or unwilling to seriously consider whether something was going wrong in their marriage and their family.

All these poor parenting scenarios are harmful to children. In each case the children cannot feel loved, accepted, or valued for themselves. The environment they are growing up in is not sufficiently safe or nurturing; there is no feeling of "home." Some children, like Jake and Alan, respond to these kinds of pressures by becoming "lightning rod" children. They attract attention in a negative way. We have even heard them hope that their misbehavior will cause their parents to come together to help them and straighten them out. (We'll discuss lightning-rod children further in chapter 4.)

All children try to make sense of the family situations they are born into in order to feel safe and loved. Children growing up in a home where the parents' marriage is rocky tend to blame themselves for their parents' arguing in an attempt to convince themselves that their parents' behavior is really caring and loving. These children don't understand that they are just pawns in the struggle between their parents.

A healthy marriage provides both a sanctuary and a buffer against the daily difficulties of life for both the adults and their children. A good marital relationship also provides give-and-take that offers a reality check for each parent. If Lena's and Heather's mothers could have sought and respected input and understanding from their husbands, their poor parenting might have been moderated, much to Lena's and Heather's benefit.

We are not suggesting that unhappy or isolated parents in dysfunctional marriages don't ever raise healthy children. In many cases, they can and do raise healthy children. Still, these parents' burdens are greater. They must provide the love, the guidance, the positive attention, the buffer, the sanctuary, and the reality check for their children, and do so without resorting to becoming excessively involved or dependent on them.

Do any of these scenarios or examples remind you of what is happening with your or your spouse's parenting? If so, you need to examine whether your parenting is faltering because of the problems in your marriage. This doesn't necessarily mean that it's time to leave. You can still take corrective action. Consider trying to talk through the situation with your spouse. If he or she is unresponsive, don't take no for an answer. Tell your spouse how serious the problems are, and that they are damaging the marriage and jeopardizing your children's well-being. Be forceful; the stakes are very high. Try talking to a clergyperson you respect, or get professional counseling. None of these measures are guarantees, but it's very important to get your parenting back on track, whether or not your marriage can be saved.

Questions to Think About

1. Do my spouse and I compete for our children's loyalty and affection? Yes___No___

2. Is one or the other of us substituting closeness with our children for the intimacy that is lacking in our marriage? Yes___No___

3. Has our home stopped being the place where we each feel emotionally safe and accepted? Yes___No___

4. Has one or both of us dropped out of the family, clearly preferring outside career and social interests to family life? Yes___No___

5. Do we play "good cop/bad cop" with our children's discipline because one of us sees the other as too harsh or too lenient? Yes___No___

6. Do I shudder when qualities I don't like in my mate surface in our children? Yes___No___

Chapter 4

How Children Falter

Step 3: Look at your children right now—Is your unhappy family affecting their school performance, behavior, and self-esteem?

During his training, Dr. Birnbach worked at a mental health clinic in a working-class neighborhood in Brooklyn, New York. One of his first patients was a fourteen-year-old boy who was referred to the clinic by his school. The boy had been caught smoking marijuana in the schoolyard. After a few of their meetings, he told Dr. Birnbach, "I was half-hoping that I'd get caught. My parents fight so much, maybe they will have to stop to help me out of this trouble."

The Lightning-Rod Child

This boy, like Jake and Alan, whom we spoke about in the previous chapter, also responded to parental discord by becoming a "lightning-rod" child. Not every child from an unhappy family becomes a lightning-rod child. Some may become depressed: the "I'm tired" child. This is the same child who, when you ask him, "What did you do today?" says, "Nothing." Many seriously underachieve without attracting too much attention to themselves. Depressed and underachieving children want to stay under the radar. By contrast, lightning-rod children crave attention and pursue it by engaging in an ever-escalating series of troubles. As they see it, since they don't feel they get much positive attention from their parents or teachers, getting negative attention is better than getting no attention at all. As Alan told us:

> When I was a kid, I felt terrible about myself. I felt I never did anything right. The only time my father noticed me was when I did things wrong.

> I never got any praise from him. My father would make a lot of derogatory comments to me, saying things like "What's the matter with you? You're never going to amount to anything." He'd complain about me to my mother—"We're wasting our time with him. Our efforts go down the toilet. What's wrong with him?" He always told me I couldn't do anything right. In my mother's eyes, a lot of the time, I couldn't do anything wrong. When I was alone with her, she'd sometimes tell me, "You can do anything you want; you can become anything you want. You have all the potential in the world, just like I did. Don't let yourself down the way I did. I didn't amount to much. Look at me—I married your father."

Alan told us that one of the ways he expressed his unhappiness was by shoplifting. Beginning around eight years old, he stole small things from local convenience stores. Once or twice he got caught, and it was brought to his parents' attention. The negative attention he received did nothing to bring his parents closer together. If anything, it made things worse between them. Alan didn't stop his shoplifting, but he did get more careful when he did it. Psychologists have studied shoplifting because of how common it is, even among adults and children in affluent families. They view shoplifting as the expression of the perpetrators' need to be repaid for the love and attention they didn't get, wished they had gotten, or are not getting. Getting things "for free" is supposed to partially satisfy that need. Michael Rutter, professor of psychiatry, Kings College, University of London, reported in the *British Journal of Psychiatry* his studies of shoplifting and other delinquent behaviors among teenage boys. He found that boys from high-conflict, intact families shoplifted more often and had a higher incidence of other delinquent behaviors than teenage boys from low-conflict, divorced families. This was irrespective of the economic and social class these boys came from.

Alan lived in an apartment building. He taught himself to make fireworks from the gunpowder from shotgun shells he shoplifted from a local sporting goods store. This was extremely dangerous. If any of the shells had exploded while he was taking them apart, he could have killed himself. On one occasion, his fireworks accidentally did go off in the stairwell of his building. The explosion made such a loud noise that several families called the police. He wasn't caught, although he partially lost the hearing in one of his ears because he was so close to the explosion.

Alan's anger about the unhappiness in his family was literally exploding out of him.

He kept attracting negative attention. In these self-sacrificial and misguided attempts to gain attention, Alan was trying to get his parents to stop fighting with each other and pay attention to him instead. His attempts failed, and things continued in this negative vein. At one point, his school guidance counselor recommended to his mother that Alan should be in counseling. His parents decided the school guidance counselor was crazy and ignored the advice. Experts agree that the greatest issue faced by troubled families and adolescents is that parents ignore the advice of professionals to seek help for their children, or they wait too long to do it. By the time they consult a professional, the problem has escalated to a crisis level.

The Crybaby

As a child, Hal reflected the unhappiness in his family in another way. Hal became a "crybaby," the young boy everyone else picked on in school. From early in his life, Hal's mother would respond in an exaggerated manner anytime he got a scratch or a bump, or when he told her that another boy had said anything cruel to him, something boys do all the time. So day after day he would come home crying from school. In response to her outsized concern—out of all proportion to the source of Hal's distress—Hal learned that he could get great sympathy and comfort from his mother for every bruise or cross word that he told her about. Over and over she soothed his tears and told him that he was "not like the other boys," that he was "much more sensitive," physically and emotionally, and that he was her favorite.

Hal tells us that, little by little, he came to believe this line of thinking. He progressively became more cautious and more fearful, stayed at home more, and retreated from his peers. Hal's mother encouraged his dependence, at least in part, because it met her needs for the companionship she was not getting in her marriage.

According to Hal, his father traveled as a salesman and was gone most of the time. As an only child, Hal was the primary focus of his mother's attentions. He was her baby. From the time he was quite small, Hal's mother would confide in him about her loneliness, her resentments toward his father, the neighbors, and various relatives.

Although it is now years later, Hal still retains a sense of personal frailty, despite being robust and in excellent health. His relationships with both men and women have continued to suffer. His feelings are still very easily hurt. Hal believes his mother's overprotection of him caused his difficulties with both men and women, including the problems in his marriage. Hal came to psychotherapy because he is unable to have a satisfying intimate relationship.

Children Learn What They Live

In study after study, researchers have found that parents' marital conflict is closely linked to children's behavioral problems. Psychologist Mavis Hetherington, whose life's work at the University of Virginia has been devoted to the impact of unhappy marriages and divorce on children, says that the single most stressful experience for any child is having two parents who argue all the time. Hetherington has studied over 2,500 children from families who are separating, divorcing, and remarrying. Even when parents don't openly argue, behavior and school performance of children from unhappy marriages suffers. Your child does not live outside your marital relationship. Even if Alan's parents had shielded him from their arguments, which they didn't, he still would have felt their anger and disrespect beneath the surface. Even if Hal's mother had not made him such an obvious substitute for her disengaged husband, Hal would have felt her isolation, loneliness, and anger.

Many couples in unhappy marriages believe that their conflict does not affect their children. Most of us assume that breaking up our marriage will be more traumatic for our children than holding even the worst marriage together. On the contrary, Abigail Stewart, psychologist and professor at the University of Michigan, in her study of 160 divorced families found no evidence that divorce is more traumatic for children than holding a bad marriage together. Stewart conducted her study in Greater Boston and published it in 1997. Each of the families in the study had at least one school-aged child between the ages of six and twelve. The study included both mothers and fathers, most of whom were the custodial parents. The sample was varied by income, education, ethnicity, religion, and reasons for divorce. The children were compared with a control group of nondivorced families.

Just contemplating divorce unleashes a torrent of guilt and fear in us.

When we consider divorce, questions about our children's futures provoke fears so great that they discourage us from even thinking about breaking up a hopelessly unhappy marriage. Children will almost always object to their parents' separating, but, as Stewart says, they will object to vaccinations, babysitters, and the first day of school as well. As she concludes, "They generally lack an understanding of the likely cost to them of depressed, angry, unhappy, or violent parents."

Peter noted that his daughter was becoming very aggressive in response to her parents' alienation from one another:

> I guess the way we were raising Sara was a mirror of everything my wife and I disagreed about, which seemed like almost everything. Even when Sara would be fresh to her mother or me, or act up because it was time to turn the TV off and eat breakfast, Helen and I would disagree. I would want to enforce some mild discipline, like a time-out—two or three minutes alone in her room—to show Sara that back talk was not acceptable. Helen would scowl, defend Sara, and in front of our seven-year-old, we would be divided. Even if Sara did go to her room, I felt the message was "Dad is the bad guy."
>
> Around the time she was eight, Sara got into physical fights with her two best friends, and her teacher contacted us to say that Sara was acting antagonistic in school. Sara was arguing with me as well. I didn't understand why she was acting this way. I guess her flare-ups made me start to question how the troubles Helen and I were having might be affecting Sara. I began to think that a child can't live day in and day out in a house where her parents are always in disagreement and not have it affect her. Still, it never occurred to me to leave the marriage because I couldn't bear the idea of losing my daily contact with Sara. I had fantasies of a better life. Who doesn't? I just took it for granted that Sara, who was my main concern, would be better off with two full-time parents. Helen and I spoke about our problems and we tried counseling, but it was probably too little, too late for us. I eventually decided it wasn't best for us to stay together at all costs. I had to leave for Sara's sake as well as my own.

When we ignore, refuse to accommodate, or behave disrespectfully and aggressively toward our spouse, we teach our children these behaviors.

Peter is a forty-five-year-old aerospace engineer. The description he gives of his home life is typical of daily life in many families. The day-to-day marriage is full of squabbles about which the parents come to little or no resolution. As we mentioned earlier, some couples disagree about money, others about extended family, child rearing, sharing household responsibilities, or combinations of these and other factors. No matter what the issues are, the disagreements persist. The children live in a war zone. It may be a hot war, in which arguments are open and frequent. It may be a cold war: Everyone knows couples who rarely raise their voices, but share a mutual dislike and disregard for one another. In either case, it's war and it's damaging to the children.

Sara rarely saw her parents resolve anything through discussion. Why, then, should we be surprised that she became argumentative with adults to try to get her way, or even used physical force with her friends? We have all heard, "Children learn what they live." Sara's high-strung behavior had its origin in her unhappy, but intact family, where her behavior gradually became a reflection of her parents' relationship. Like most people, Peter stayed in the marriage for several reasons, most prominently deep concerns about his daughter's well-being, but equally important, fears of financial ruin and of being alone.

Another way that children commonly show their distress and anger in an unhappy family is by seriously underperforming in school. Recently, the National Institute of Mental Health, a U.S. government agency, funded a three-year study of two hundred children aged six and older. Conducted at the Hospital at Johnson City Medical Center at East Tennessee State University, the study analyzed children's behavior, attention span, ability to focus at home and in school, as well as how the children perceived their parents' relationship. Kids who worried about their parents' conflicts had more difficulties in school, frequently because they could not pay attention. Researchers attributed this to concerns the children have about their parents that increase their anxiety, depression, and aggression and impair their ability to relate well to other children.

Getting a poor start in school usually has repercussions for a lifetime. When the school labels a child as a poor performer, that label increasingly becomes a self-fulfilling prophecy. The child gets tracked into classes for low achievers and troubled kids. Oftentimes, teachers' expectations of children in these classes are low. The kids in these classes see one another as poor performers and troublemakers, so their self-esteem suffers. Sometimes we've heard them refer to themselves as "losers." This is the extreme. Even more common are children whose parents receive feedback from their teachers about how bright they are, but how they put no effort into their schoolwork and fail to achieve anywhere near their potential. Alan's situation reflected this reaction.

From his earliest days in school, Alan was known as an underperformer. His teachers continuously told his parents that he had great potential but didn't live up to it. He felt teachers were singling him out and picking on him. When one of his teachers would tell him to stop talking, he would get defensive, and deny the behavior, convincing himself that the teacher was being unfair. He talked out of turn in class. He didn't adequately complete his homework or prepare for tests, except sometimes in science, which he liked.

At home, as we have seen, Alan's parents were unpredictable and inconsistent, except in their ongoing disagreements with each other. While his mother would sometimes tell Alan that he could do anything he set his mind to, she would also tell him that his sister was much smarter, and that Alan probably had the lowest IQ in their family. His father, you will recall, was more consistently negative in his feedback to Alan. Despite his poor grades in school, Alan competed on a test to get into a special science high school in eighth grade. He earned one of the highest scores out of thousands of children, and gained admission to the school. However, during his first year, he failed half his courses. His entire school career mirrored the inconsistency in the parenting he received. To put it in his own words: "What went on at home caused me to believe that I was a loser in school, and what went on at school reinforced the lousy feedback I got at home."

Alan's sister, designated as the family genius, fared even worse. While, ultimately, Alan was able to graduate from college and secure a good job, he told us, his sister's life has been marked by even greater inconsistencies and unpredictability than Alan's, one year booming, the next year failure.

Opposing Philosophies

There are so many ways in which kids from unhappy families reflect the family's problems in their behavior and school performance, we cannot catalogue all of them. Hal's, Sara's, Alan's, Lena's, and Jake's problems all go back to their earliest months and years of life. Because parenting and consistent expectations falter from the beginning, babies and young children often develop sleep difficulties, cry excessively, and have numerous tantrums. If the father, for example, believes the baby should cry himself to sleep, and the mother cannot tolerate this, in a happy couple the two will reach an accommodation that satisfies both and sends a clear and consistent message to the baby.

In an unhappy couple, this is likely to become a source of conflict, with each of the parents hardening their point of view. The baby will be given conflicting and inconsistent messages when it's time to go to sleep, sometimes reflecting the dad's wishes, sometimes the mom's. Such contradictory guidance and parental inconsistency confuse the child and teach him to try to manipulate his parents. The child's philosophy becomes, "If I can't get my way with Mom, I'll try Dad, and I won't tell him Mom already said no."

Differences in parental philosophy can center around eating, playing with siblings, school study habits, obedience, punishments, setting limits—almost anything. The point is that the inability of an unhappy couple to genuinely agree creates multiple problems for their children. Sadly, the conflict is not usually about the children, but about the parents and their failure to agree about many issues affecting parenting. When the child behaves in a way that displeases either one of his parents, the child is blamed, confusing him and damaging his feelings about himself. Multiply this hundreds of times over many years. Ask yourself if some version of this pattern is happening in your household. Should you be getting help to sort this out? Along with many other researchers, Mavis Hetherington at the University of Virginia has compared children in thousands of households for decades. She has repeatedly found that children in single-parent households, where there is consistent and loving parenting, do better in almost every way than children in unhappy intact households where the parents have unresolved and contradictory philosophies on child rearing.

Questions to Think About

1. Can I think of any recent incidents in which one of our children has called attention to himself by getting into trouble, or in some other negative way? Yes___No___
2. Do I blame our child's repeated misbehavior, in or out of school, on the child, my spouse, or on myself, and never look at these problems as a symptom of the struggles in our marriage? Yes___No___
3. Do I feel it is possible that the conflict in our marriage could indirectly be causing misbehavior or lowered school performance in our children? Yes___No___
4. Am I becoming convinced that two full-time parents who agree on little fail to offer as wholesome an environment for children as a stable, low-conflict, single-parent home? Yes___No___

CHAPTER 5

How Sex and Intimacy Falter

Step 4: Face the truth—What is the quality of our sexual and intimate life?

Mary Beth tells us that she argues with her husband Ken about their sex life. She feels they aren't intimate often enough; he says he has less frequent need for sex than she does. Her husband makes her feel that her need for more sex is her problem, not his or theirs. This leaves her feeling rejected, sad, and angry.

Nancy told us that she never says "no" to her husband Marvin, because he has a temper and gets angry and sullen if she isn't in the mood. He also controls what they do sexually, and how they do it. Nancy says she sometimes feels he is too controlling, but she goes along with him anyway. She also admits that she wishes his touch were gentler, but feels she can't talk to him about it.

Sam says his wife says "no" to him most of the time he tries to initiate sex. He feels hurt and humiliated when she calls him a "pervert" because, at age forty, he would like to have sex a couple of times a week. She even discourages him from hugging her because she says every time he hugs her, he wants to have sex with her. His protests fall on deaf ears.

Ron's wife refuses to make love with him spontaneously, but says she is willing to make a date to have sex. She is generally unavailable weeknights, but will usually agree to a prearranged weekend night. In fact, when Saturday comes, she reminds him that they are supposed to have sex that night. When they have sex, Ron often feels that she can't wait for it to be over.

Physical intimacy in a marriage is a barometer of what's going on in the rest of the relationship. What's happening in the bedroom is connected with what's happening outside the bedroom.

It's each person's responsibility to meet the other partner's needs reliably and enjoyably.

Sex Is a Barometer

A sexual relationship is a form of communication, and, like any good communication, there needs to be give-and-take. Each member of a couple bears some responsibility for wholeheartedly taking part in the communication, even if, at first, they are not in the mood. In the United States, most married couples have sex once or twice a week, depending on their age. Even once every few weeks is fine, if it is genuinely acceptable to both of you. This doesn't only include having sexual intercourse. Physical intimacy can be expressed in many ways.

Work and parenting stress, anxiety about money and job security, and fatigue caused by overwork and worry all drain some of the energy that might otherwise encourage a more vibrant sex life for a couple. Americans work longer hours than people in any other society, and the number of hours we work continues to increase every year. This is why when most couples are away on vacation they often find they have sex more frequently, because the stress levels and the day-to-day grind of life is so much lower. Sex is a need, like hunger or sleep. Under adverse conditions, you can go with very little sleep for quite a while, or live on a starvation diet. It's similar with sex. However, your relationship pays a price for not meeting your or your partner's needs for sex and affection over the long haul.

Solitary viewing of pornography and visits to Internet chat rooms for online sexual communication are some of the ways people in unhappy marriages try to satisfy their needs for sexual excitement and release. It's fairly well known that, with the easy access on the Internet, there has been a huge increase in these activities among both men and women—including married men and women in large numbers. This is a sad testament to avoidance of real intimacy with one's mate. *Divorce* magazine reports that more than half of married men who engage in online sexual communication or telephone sex feel there is nothing "unfaithful" about their behavior. On the other hand, couples who occasionally view pornography together may find that it enhances their sexual intimacy, if both are comfortable with it.

In this same vein, many perfectly healthy married men depend on performance-enhancing drugs, such as Viagra, to perform sexually with their wives because their hearts aren't in it. Most of these married men are unable to have sex with their wives without using these drugs. Of course, we are not referring to men with physical ailments, like diabetes or hypertension, or those experiencing the aftermath of prostate surgery or other conditions that influence their ability to have and sustain an erection.

Women are not immune to sexual dysfunction in marriage, either. A recent study by Dr. Jan Shifrin of Massachusetts General Hospital, involving more than 31,000 married women, shows that 44 percent of them reported marital sexual problems, most particularly feeling little or no desire to have sex with their husbands. While many of the women said they didn't care, almost all said their husbands were terribly troubled by this.

The spouses we introduced at the beginning of the chapter didn't feel it was their responsibility to look out for their mate's sexual well-being and contentment. Not feeling responsible for your mate's sexual satisfaction, not feeling any desire for intimate contact or for the expression of affection toward your mate—these problems signal deeper divisions between you, such as breakdowns in your communication and love for each other.

The 75 Percent Rule

One question to ask yourself is how often you and your spouse say "no" or make an excuse to not respond to your partner's desire for sex. In relatively happy marriages, partners tend to say "yes" to an overture to make love at least 75 percent of the time. This gives people the freedom to say "no" occasionally, if it's really not a good time for them, and to do it without building resentment or making their partner feel rejected. You need to be able to count on your partner in a marriage in many ways: to live up to financial commitments, to live up to the loyalty you've pledged to one another, to live up to the responsibilities of daily living—and also to live up to reliably being loving and a lover.

If every conversation between you and your spouse were held in the same place, about the same few subjects, in the same order, at the same time on the same day, you'd die of boredom.

In a solid marriage, it is up to you to listen to or figure out what your partner's sexual and affectional needs are, and to reliably respond to them, unless your partner is seeking something harmful, unreasonable, or beyond your ability. Sometimes what is in and what is out of bounds can be difficult to negotiate. What's unreasonable for one person may not be for the other. When two people come together, at whatever stage of life, they bring different ideas of what is sexy, what is permissible, and what is unreasonable. If one person is constantly stifling the other's suggestions, the more inhibited person is too much in control. Good sexual communication, like good verbal communication, requires spontaneity and openness to new ideas. If every conversation between you and your spouse were held in the same place, about the same few subjects, in the same order, at the same time on the same day, you'd die of boredom. You and your spouse need to be able to count on and be open to each other. It's a partnership. If this isn't happening in your marriage, there's a big hole in it, and you have to figure out how, and if, you can fix it.

Bonnie and John did just that. They had been married for five years. There had been a powerful attraction between them, and lots of passion. Like all couples, the novelty and some of the heat in their sexual relationship diminished after the honeymoon period. As some of the excitement was wearing off, Bonnie got into the habit of not being receptive unless she was totally "in the mood." This meant that she rejected John's overtures more and more frequently. For John, it seemed that she was saying "no" to him much more often than "yes." In her mind, she had a good reason every time, but each time she said "no" he experienced it as another small rejection. Like the proverbial Chinese water torture, the little rejections added up, bit by bit. John came to expect to be rejected and therefore reached out less and less, until virtually the only times they were intimate with each other were when Bonnie initiated sex. John would almost always say "yes."

Bonnie didn't like that. She told us: "I didn't fall in love with a passive man. I fell in love with a passionate one who wants me, and who makes me feel desired and beautiful. He was not doing that anymore." John protested that most of the times he had taken the initiative, Bonnie had said "no." So he had essentially given up.

This would be a great story if we could say that this single conversation fixed the problem. It didn't. Some variation of this conversation had to take place numerous times. Sometimes there were bruised feelings and defensiveness, but over a period of more than a year, Bonnie became aware of how often she had been saying "no" to John. Even then the problem wasn't solved. John was still wary of being rejected, and often refrained from initiating sex because he wasn't willing to risk a "no" from Bonnie. Sometimes he got it into his head that even though she said "yes" she didn't really want to make love, and was just placating him.

The majority of sexual problems result from emotional estrangement and unresolved issues in a marriage.

Sex, of course, works best when both people want it. Over time, Bonnie really changed. She learned that she didn't have to be totally "in the mood." If she just participated, she would usually get in the mood, even if she were tired, shut down, grouchy, or preoccupied. If she went along with it, a little bit of affection from John would change her mood for the better within a few minutes. Bonnie found out that she was not just being dutiful. She came to see that the enhanced frequency, ease, and communication about sex provided comfort, relaxation, and both emotional and physical pleasure for her and John, and most importantly, that it deepened their love for one another.

There's a subtext in this story that we need to pay attention to. Bonnie and John each have a big investment in wanting their marriage to work well. They share many good things together and agree for the most part on the nine areas couples need to work out. This was an area that was starting to show signs of deterioration, and, with effort, mutual commitment, and good communication, they were able to get it back on track.

Sex is Fragile

The sexual communication in a marriage is fragile. When it breaks, it is very hard to fix. It's just as likely that a man might initiate the breakdown in sexual communication as a woman. Men get just as preoccupied, fatigued, resistant, and likely to withdraw from sex as women do. John told us that it was more than a year after Bonnie started saying "yes" before he really felt comfortable spontaneously initiating physical intimacy with his wife, as he had in the early days of their marriage. He was surprised at how shut down he had become.

Impotence and premature ejaculation for men, failure to have orgasms for men or women, and a lack of interest in sex are all symptoms of trouble in the sexual communication between husband and wife—except in cases where there are medical problems. All these sexual symptoms should first be evaluated by a physician. If your spouse suffers from sexual dysfunction, you need to encourage her to get checked out. Her refusal to get checked out by a physician, however embarrassing it may be for her, is another way of refusing to accept responsibility for the sexual communication in your marriage.

Sex Is Glue

Sex is a kind of glue in a marriage; it holds the couple together through bad times as well as good. Without sexual intimacy, there is a danger that in times of difficulty the couple can come unglued. If the glue isn't holding, a space may begin to grow between the couple. It's worth repeating from family therapist Eleanor Craig-Green: No one can come between a husband and wife, unless there is already a space. It's hard to find reliable statistics on how many husbands and wives currently have, or have had, sex outside their marriages. Many won't admit to it, even in anonymous surveys. In the *Journal of Couple and Relationship Therapy*, J. D. Attwood and Lynn Schwartz, two of the most prominent researchers on Internet infidelity, report that the best estimates are that as many as 40 percent of married women and 60 percent of married men have been unfaithful to their partner at least one time during their marriage. In *After the Affair*, Dr. Janice Spring says that one or the other spouse has been involved in an affair in more than 40 percent of couples.

Dangerous Times

Marriage counselors talk about three perilous periods in marriages:

- Two years
- Twelve years
- Twenty years

Two Years

A large number of people wake up after around two years of marriage, the end of the so-called honeymoon period, and discover that they have little in common with each other. The old adage says that "Opposites attract." Indeed, they often do—initially. A problem with being married to your "opposite" is that once the initial hot attraction wears off, the two of you have to live with the little you have in common. You may not share the same friends, interests, goals, or even values. Rather than waiting to complicate their lives with children and with mortgages, some people in this situation begin to question whether they should stay together.

Winona and Carl have been married for three years. They are in their late twenties, but Winona pointed out that they rarely have sex with each other any more. In fact, it seems they share few interests or activities together. When Winona complains about their lack of intimacy, Carl puts her off by telling her he's too tired because of stress from work. Recently, when they were out shopping together, Carl slipped away, presumably to go to the men's room. After a few minutes, Winona saw him making a purchase. She saw him put a small box in his pocket. Delighted, she assumed it was a gift for her, and that it was meant to be a surprise.

The next day, when she saw that the package was gone from the drawer Carl had put it in, she e-mailed him: "I thought you bought that gift for me. Did you bring it to work to give to Lorrie?" He wrote back: "You have some nerve spying on me. Anyway, you know Lorrie is my assistant. She does so much for me at work, of course I should show her some appreciation. I'm very busy right now; I can't talk about this anymore." When they spoke later, Winona told him that she was hurt and angry because, if the gift was only meant as a sign of work-related appreciation, why had Carl hidden the gift from her? Winona recounted this incident in therapy and again lamented how the sexual relationship between her and Carl had deteriorated.

There is a fast-growing space between Carl and Winona. She confronted Carl about whether he was having an affair with Lorrie. Although he denied it, Winona never fully believed him, but felt there was little else she could say. Whether or not Carl is lying, there is still a serious problem. The doubts that linger in his wife's mind cause the distance between her and Carl to grow even larger as trust breaks down between them.

Twelve Years

At around twelve years of marriage, there is the high potential of a spike in marital discontent. This is at a time when couples are absorbed in work, raising their children, and managing their households. Weekends are often spent performing routine chores and following the children in their activities, such as Little League and soccer. In many families, the wife takes one child to soccer, while the husband takes the other to Little League. In the afternoon, the wife takes both kids with her when she goes to the supermarket, while the husband does the chores in the yard. Seemingly, this

It should come as no surprise that many extramarital affairs have started at soccer and Little League games.

is all for the sake of efficiency, but the result is that the couple winds up spending little time with each other on the weekend. The daily exhaustion of each weekday is compounded by these obligations and separations on weekends. After twelve years of this routine, the romantic and social relationship between husband and wife has often become completely lost. Each feels lonely for energetic, enthusiastic, adult attention. This is a dangerous time in a marriage.

When a marriage is going through a difficult time, any of us can feel a little victimized, neglected, old, and underappreciated. We may not feel very good about ourselves. We may even feel a little desperate. We may feel angry and alienated, and in need of appreciation and excitement. This is when we say to ourselves: "Is this all there is?" All this makes some people very vulnerable to flattering attention from a member of the opposite sex who is not your spouse.

Twenty Years

The third perilous time for marriages is around your twentieth anniversary. The children have left, or are leaving for college, or to set off on their own lives. Suddenly, the nest is empty and the two of you are thrown together, on your own for the first time since the early days of your marriage. For your marriage to survive this time, you need to have kept your intimate relationship and sense of companionship alive and vital. You need to have mutual interests, some social life in common, adequate sexual communication, and an appreciation and respect for each other that includes what the two of you have accomplished together over all these years.

Bridget and Lou had lost their romance, their sex life, and their intimate connection over the years of raising their children. As soon as Bridget and Lou's youngest son left the house to go to college, they knew they had to do something to counteract the empty nest. They started going out every night (really!). Through her business, Bridget made friends with a wealthy older man and his wife. The older couple had an exciting and glamorous life, into which they welcomed Bridget and Lou.

The two couples socialized extensively. Both the husband and wife in the older couple separately confided in Bridget how unhappy they were in their marriage. It also increasingly became obvious to Bridget that many of the friends in their new social circle were unfaithful in their marriages, disrespectful to their spouses, drank too much, or had issues with their children. Bridget told us she had finally gone for psychotherapy because she felt quite depressed about her life, despite the social whirl she was in. Fairly early in their conversations, her therapist observed that the older man was acting in some ways like "half of a husband" to Bridget. She observed, "You have two men in your life, each one acting like half of a husband. It doesn't seem they add up to anything." A few years later, Bridget and Lou divorced. They had nothing left inside their marriage, and looking for a transfusion from outside their marriage just seems to have hastened the end.

Avoiding Trouble

Research psychologist Joseph Forgas of Florida State University has found that when married people in happy marriages meet people of the opposite sex whom they find attractive, they instinctively feel a little uncomfortable and briefly look away. They avoid establishing close contact with an attractive person who isn't their mate. If you believe you already have your best partner, you avoid establishing a close connection with somebody else. Conversely, many people in unhappy marriages spontaneously behave the same way single people do, and are naturally responsive to members of the opposite sex they find attractive.

Insurance Policies

In unhappy marriages, one or the other partner may have one or more attractive opposite-sex friends who could conceivably become romantic partners in other circumstances. We call these relationships "insurance policies," because they provide potential backup in case the marriage breaks down. The so-called "office wife," a colleague at work who a man or woman shares a highly dependent and intense relationship with, is one version of this, but not the only one. Sometimes these relationships are long-standing and even precede the marriage.

We've encountered many of them: the man who claims he is happily married but text messages his ex-girlfriend several times a day; the woman whose best buddy is a male colleague she sometimes travels with for business and whom her husband strongly resents; Carl, who has developed a powerful, confidential relationship with his coworker Lorrie, the young married woman who won't make a move without first consulting her

Each of us has a limited amount of intimacy to spread around. If you give this intimacy to someone other than your spouse, you drain at least some of it from your marriage.

If you think something in the intimate relationship between you is wrong, it is.

charming older male mentor. All may claim that these relationships are innocent and swear that sex never enters into the equation. That's okay, but it's not good enough. Sexual intimacy is critical in a marriage, but it's not the only kind of intimacy that is necessary to make a marriage thrive. Ann, whose story opened this book, had a relatively active sex life with her husband almost until the day he left her. It turned out that he had been having an affair for several years. While he and Ann had sex together, what was lacking in their marriage was any kind of emotional intimacy, something that Ann was painfully aware of.

Affairs Destroy Marriages

Oftentimes, it might seem to be easier to begin a sexual affair than to try to work things out with your spouse. This is usually a mistake if you want to keep your marriage intact. In an affair, you are getting crucial intimate needs met outside the marriage. This widens the distance between you and your spouse, whether or not she knows about the affair. If she doesn't know about it, the deception builds a barrier between you because you have a big secret, and may even feel somewhat condescending to your spouse, who is in the dark. If your partner does find out about the affair, it creates an even greater barrier. The trust between you may be permanently broken by the betrayal. Once trust is shattered, it will never be restored to its original level of comfort and security. Doubt will always be a factor.

Press Your Case

A successful marriage needs intimacy. If, like the people we have described, you feel you can't speak to your partner intimately, or that your partner isn't interested when you try to speak with her, you need to address the problem. As strange as it sounds, you need to talk to your partner about not being able to talk to her, and to let her know how serious this situation is. Again we urge you to tell her that you are reading this book.

Intimacy requires taking chances and making yourself vulnerable. You need to be able to say, "This hurts me," "This makes me feel rejected," or "I feel you prefer this other person's interest in you over mine." Many people are afraid of intimacy and don't feel comfortable being this close or personal, even in their marriage. This discomfort may be cultural, or it may be developed from long-standing habits in childhood. Ask your partner to open up to you. What prevents her from confiding in you? Don't be satisfied with a response like this: "Nothing is wrong. It's just work-related." Don't let your conversation end there. She's probably afraid of opening up about her feelings for fear they will be hurt. She may worry about hurting your feelings, or, most simply, she may not be examining her own feelings deeply enough. If you don't feel responded to, tell your partner her lack of response is unacceptable. You need to be able to say this several times if your partner doesn't respond the first time.

In defining the unhappy marriage, we have described the nine areas that all couples must resolve together in order to have a successful marriage. Subsequently, we wrote about how, if parenting is faltering, this is a sign of serious marital problems, but not necessarily a sign that it is time to go—with effort, your joint parenting can improve. Similarly, if sex and emotional intimacy are faltering, it is a serious sign of problems in your relationship. If you answered "yes" to many of the questions at the end of the first three chapters, and now answer "yes" to many of the questions at the end of this chapter, we feel you should certainly be concerned about the serious problems in your marriage. Does this mean it is time to go? Maybe. What measures have you tried to fix the problem so far? What have you not tried? We've been encouraging you to talk to your spouse, and to seek the advice of a counselor and/or a clergyperson. We don't encourage you to talk this over with friends or relatives at this point, especially if you haven't spoken to your spouse first. That would be very disloyal of you. Additionally, the advice of friends and relatives tends to be unreliable and influenced by their love for you. They tend to tell you what they think you want to hear.

We know this isn't easy. We know we are asking you to answer hard questions. We know you are unhappy. We are encouraging you not to put your head in the sand. One way or the other we want you to minimize your long-term suffering by getting at the problems now.

Questions to Think About

1. As a barometer of our marriage, is our sex life indicating that the climate is too cool? Yes___No___

2. Does one of us say "no" to a sexual overture from the other more than 25 percent of the time? Yes___No___
3. Are we unable to talk about our sex life? Yes___No___
4. Do our weekends revolve almost entirely around household responsibilities, taking our children to activities, and socializing with other adults, with little or no time spent just with each other? Yes___No___
5. Is one or both of us susceptible to the attractiveness of others because we no longer feel we are with our best possible partner? Yes___No___
6. Does one of us have an opposite-sex friend who provides either sexual or nonsexual intimacy we don't have in our marriage? Yes___No___
7. Are most of the couples or singles we socialize with unhappily married or divorced? Yes___No___

Chapter 6

How Physical and Mental Health Falter

Step 5: Assess—Is marital stress affecting my physical and mental health? My children's? My spouse's?

Marsha's dentist was shocked when she came for her annual checkup. "What's going on in your life?" he asked. "You have developed terrible periodontal problems in such a short time." Marsha was only twenty-seven at the time, a very young age for rapid gum deterioration. What had been happening in the course of the year since Marsha had seen her dentist was that the level of marital discord between her and her husband had escalated dramatically. Her dentist, just by looking at her gums, immediately recognized that her level of stress had to have vastly increased since her last checkup.

Similarly, in the last few years of Crystal's marriage to Gil, she told us she developed severe itching and rashes. She went from one allergist to another, and was tested again and again for various allergens, with no conclusive results. She had everything in her house dry-cleaned or sterilized; she bought an expensive humidifier on the advice of one doctor. She started being very careful about what she ate, eliminating first one and then another potential source of the allergic reaction—all to no avail. After a conversation about what was going on in her life, her long-time family physician, a close family friend, half-seriously said to her, "Do you think you could be allergic to your husband?" They laughed, but Crystal's itches and rashes persisted until around the time her divorce became final, about two years after she and Gil had separated. She told us that the itches have since gone away and have never returned.

Stress Becomes Physical

Both Marsha's and Crystal's physical symptoms are examples of how some people turn marital stress in their lives into very real physical problems.

The connection between the mind and the body has been written about for centuries. The connection between stress, especially from unhappy marriages, and various physical ailments has been proven in research conducted in recent years. The list of illnesses associated with the stress of unhappy marriage is considerable and no one really speaks about it. Of course, there may be numerous other stresses in someone's life that can contribute to any of these illnesses. In the same way that poor marriages work against physical and mental health, a good marriage can provide protection.

In his book *Why Marriages Succeed or Fail,* John Gottman of the University of Pennsylvania noted that stress-related illness is more prevalent among people in unhappy marriages. Gottman and many other researchers catalogue the connection between stress and increased incidence of the following conditions:

- high blood pressure
- stomach ulcers
- asthma
- arthritis
- obesity
- periodontal disease
- sleep problems

After a couple argues, wounds take 40 percent longer to heal.

Additional recent research has shown that chronic and frequent marital disagreements are linked to an increased risk of heart disease and type 2 diabetes. Couples who report that they are in unhappy marriages have a higher incidence of the flu, the common cold, allergies, headaches, and chronic diarrhea. Married men in poor-quality marriages showed worse immune-system response in a study by psychologist Janice Kiecolt-Glaser, conducted at Ohio State University College of Medicine. The speed of heart patients' recovery is also linked to the quality of their marriages. Among the elderly, people who have more negative feelings toward their spouses are almost twice as likely to die of heart disease within four years than those who have more positive feelings toward their spouses. Women who have arthritis and/or lower back pain, and who experience their spouses as critical of them, report higher levels of pain than women with the same ailments who report that their spouses are supportive.

In one landmark study done at the University of Michigan, over four thousand postal workers were asked about marital stress and their health. First they rated their marriages as either "happy" or "unhappy." Those who rated their marriages as "unhappy" then reported more than twice the number of all the illnesses we mentioned when compared with those in the study who rated their marriages as "happy." In a follow-up study five years later, a number of the postal workers who had initially rated their marriages as "unhappy" had divorced or separated. Some were single, and some had remarried. When the ones who were separated or divorced were asked to evaluate their health again, the frequency of formerly reported illnesses had dropped. Yes, they got healthier once they were out of their unhappy marriages. They now reported a similar frequency of illness as the "happily married" participants in the original study.

In an initial interview, one of Dr. Birnbach's patients, Arlene, a thirty-year-old woman, wondered: "I can't understand why I'm so unhappy. I come from such a close-knit family." Later in the interview, when he asked about the health of her family, she said, "We're all very healthy, although my mother suffers from high blood pressure and my father has stomach ulcers; actually, his arthritis sometimes puts him flat on his back in bed for a week. I don't know if you consider a weight problem a health issue, but everyone in our family is overweight. I also get frequent headaches. I guess you can say we do have our fair share of health problems." Several years later, Arlene reminded Dr. Birnbach of this conversation. She told him that this talk had gotten her to open her eyes to the stress in her family and the unhappiness in her parents' marriage.

What's going on with your physical health? What about your spouse's and your children's health? Like Arlene, maybe you have never thought about it before. You probably didn't realize that the frequent or chronic stomachaches, colds, flus, backaches, headaches, or overeating that you or your family experience are much more common in families with unhappy marriages. (It also works the other way around: Frequent chronic illnesses also put stress on individuals and marriages, complicating the picture.) This doesn't mean you should divorce if you or others in your family suffer all-too-frequent illness caused by the stress, conflict, and alienation in your marriage. It means you have to pay attention to your marriage. You have to take these physical symptoms as a signal of the mind-body connection and a wake-up call to address the issues in your marriage that may be contributing to your physical symptoms. When the mind is unhappy, the body may suffer. When the mind is unhappy, mental health may also suffer. In the research on the postal workers, psychological problems, such as depression, lack of energy, irritability, feelings of hopelessness, and lowered self-esteem, were also more prevalent when the subjects were in unhappy marriages than after they divorced.

Food As a Substitute for Love

Ann, whom you'll recall from the Introduction, dreamed about living in an empty house, tried to remedy the emptiness and loneliness she felt in her marriage and from her husband's workaholism by filling up with food. When her kids were asleep and she was alone, which was most nights, she'd consume bags of potato chips, and stuff herself with anything chocolate as she sat in front of the television. She gained fifty pounds (23kg) doing this. The food wasn't enough to fill Ann's emotional emptiness; in fact, the more weight she gained, the worse she felt about herself.

Her children were not enough either, even though she was very involved with them. And, of course, she got almost nothing from her marriage. A sign of Ann's deteriorating mental health was that she began accumulating sleeping pills that had been prescribed to counteract her sleeping problems. She was so desperate about her unhappy, empty marriage that she entertained vague ideas of committing suicide. Persistent thoughts of suicide are a serious sign of deterioration of judgment and mental health. Fortunately for Ann, her husband decided it was time to leave the marriage and she was released from the empty house and the relationship that had been her emotional prison. After a difficult year of readjustment, she is doing more with her life. She has built an active social network and is dating a man who is much more attentive to her.

Drugs and Alcohol

Drug and alcohol dependencies are also a physical sign of emotional distress. Sid was in therapy, and he repeatedly tried to talk with his wife, Marilyn, about her anger and her lack of sexual responsiveness. He also suggested that they go into couples counseling, but he couldn't get anywhere with her. At a party on a business trip, he tried cocaine. It lifted his spirits and made him feel better than he'd felt in years. He began using cocaine more and more, even while he still tried to encourage his wife to get help with him for their marriage. Eventually, he started using cocaine at home. Not surprisingly, Sid's drug use alarmed Marilyn. It became his way of saying, "If you don't pay attention to me, and agree to get help, I'll just withdraw from you." Not only did this not work with her, but Sid was arrested trying to buy cocaine and lost his job.

Premature Aging

We hadn't seen our friend Phil in about five years. He had gone to school with us, and then he married and moved away to a distant suburb. When he called and suggested that we have lunch, because he was going to be in the city and hoped to interest us in a business idea he had, we jumped at the chance. We were taken aback when Phil came into the office. In the five years since we had last seen him, he looked like he had aged fifteen years. He had gained a lot of weight. He was hunched over. He was pale, and he looked haggard. When we talked, he seemed to have lost much of his former self-confidence. We rapidly felt that, in contrast to the person we once knew, this was someone with whom we certainly didn't want to go into a business venture. Eventually, we asked him what was going on his life; Phil told us he was in a pretty unhappy marriage. He certainly looked miserable.

Children's Mental and Physical Health

Children in families with unhappy marriages also have greater emotional and physical health problems. In a study of ninety-three first-time mothers and their infants, when the babies were six and nine months old, the babies showed deteriorating physical health and decreased ability to regulate their emotions when their parents were engaged in a high level of marital conflict, according to Christopher Porter and M. Woulden-Miller in their study done in 2003 at Brigham Young University. Dr. John Gottman and Linda Katz, working at the University of Washington in 1993 published a similar study, showing that children's health and relationships with other children were negatively affected by marital conflict. Mavis Hetherington at the University of Virginia found that children are better off in single-parent households that are stable than in unhappy, intact families. Her study is considered the most definitive that has been done in this field. It lasted over thirty years and involved more than fourteen hundred families. In her research, Hetherington discovered that children in stable single-parent homes generally have about half the number of physical, emotional, and school-related problems, compared with children who live in unhappy marriages.

Kim is fifteen. Her mental health is deteriorating; she is self-destructive. She recently stole her parents' car, met up with some friends, drank beer, and crashed into another vehicle. She and the three other teenagers who were in her parents' car, as well as two people in the other car, were all hurt in the collision. Fortunately, no one was seriously injured. For Kim, this is the most recent in a string of problem behaviors going back a number of years. She has been suspended from school. She is defiant toward her parents. She has used drugs, and apparently is very sexually active. It appears that for their entire marriage, Kim's parents have had too little involvement with one another or with Kim. Her father, who is a successful businessman, works very long hours and travels almost every week for work. He seems to go through the motions of being involved with both his wife and Kim, but is not involved with either one.

Last year, Kim had an important role in a school play. Her father put things in his life aside so that he could go to the production, but at the last minute got caught up in a meeting, rushed to get to the play, but missed Kim's part entirely. After the show, he tried to cover this up when Kim asked him some questions about his reactions to her performance, but she caught him in his lies. His wife also complains that when they are together he is always preoccupied with everything else but her.

Kim's mom is a stay-at-home mother. She sleeps late and spends much of her time with female friends, shopping, taking classes in watercolor painting, and working out at the gym. She has been having an affair with the husband of one of the family's friends. Kim told us that she came home early from school one day when she was nine, and found her mother and the family friend kissing in the living room. Her mother told Kim he was her "special friend," but not to tell her father about him.

Blaming the Children

With so much to cope with, no wonder Kim is a very troubled girl. She is neglected by both her parents, and burdened by the pain of her parents' lies and lives. Kim's parents should not ignore what her behavior signifies for all of them. Her behavior didn't cause her parents' estrangement and self-absorption; rather, it is the other way around. The difficulty is in getting her parents to acknowledge that. When you talk to Kim's parents, they want to blame their daughter for her own problems, and leave it at that. When you talk to Kim, you hear her admitting, "Yes, I'm all screwed up, but both of my parents are crazy, too. They are both locked in their own lives, and I'm walking around with this stupid secret about my mother. My father screams at me for smoking pot, when I know he smokes it, too." The outlook for Kim's future is not bright. Things have gone way too far. Her parents' abdication of their responsibilities has been severe, and Kim has been giving signals of her distress for years. Her parents needed to recognize the unwholesome environment they began creating when Kim was ten and she first began getting into trouble. At that time, they were too estranged to take unified, consistent, and persistent action—and they still are. It would help Kim if they could become serious about trying to put their marriage back together. Alternatively, divorce might not be a bad decision. However, it would not benefit Kim if it became a contentious divorce and the alienation between her parents escalated into open conflict.

David can't stop complaining about his seven-year-old son Brad. It's true that Brad throws temper tantrums and is frequently disobedient. Brad calls himself a dummy, and doesn't do most things he is supposed to do with much competence. If he is cleaning his dishes off the table after dinner, he spills food on the floor. He won't put his toys away. He lies about whether he has homework. This infuriates David, and frightens Sandy, Brad's mother. She worries constantly about Brad. What neither David nor Sandy seems willing to acknowledge or understand is that their son's behavior probably reflects the discord between them, especially about how they parent Brad. The more David acts harshly toward their son, the more Sandy pampers Brad and fails to set standards for his behavior. Brad's poor self-image and poor behavior are likely the fruit of problems in their marriage. Of course, it is possible that Brad's problems are caused by other factors, such as hyperactivity, or frustration brought on by a learning disability, and a competent evaluation should assess these other possibilities. Such physically based problems are common and can certainly cause or exacerbate marital problems.

For adults and children, there is a serious cost to physical and emotional health from the stress of living in an unhappy marriage. The connection between marital distress and children's deteriorating mental and physical health and school performance has been repeatedly demonstrated in numerous studies. The worst solution for everyone is the status quo, ignoring the indications that things aren't right. You need to evaluate which of the nine areas are causing conflict between you and your spouse. What can you do about the situation? How can you get the marriage moving in the right direction? This is the issue that Kim's parents and Brad's parents are faced with, although at present, they all seem unable to acknowledge the problem. Maybe Kim's recent car crash will stimulate her parents to look hard at what role their neglected and alienated marriage has played in Kim's out-of-control behavior. So far, nothing we have tried has gotten through to David and Sandy about the effect of their marital problems on Brad. Whether you argue openly, or are alienated and have given up with no resolution, the stress that comes along with your unhappy marriage takes an enormous physical and mental toll on both you and your children.

So what are the signals in your mental or physical health—or in that of your spouse or children—that suggest you have marriage problems? Kim, Ann, and Greg's stories are vivid and extreme. Marsha, Crystal, Arlene, and Phil's stories are less so. You shouldn't have to go to extreme lengths of stress-induced physical and mental illness before you acknowledge that your marriage is in trouble. One person told us that it took a serious injury in an automobile accident to get her to realize how unhappy she was in her marriage. Another told us he took a terrible fall in his home, breaking several ribs and an arm. Both told us that during the healing process, while they were asking themselves how such a catastrophe could have happened to them, they realized how desperate they were in their marriages, and became motivated to do something about the problem.

Questions to Think About

1. Is it possible that my lack of energy, sleep problems, irritability, lack of enthusiasm, or depression is a result of our unhappy marriage? Yes___No___
2. Does anyone in our family overeat compulsively; suffer from obesity, anorexia, or bulimia; or use alcohol, drugs, or mood-altering medications excessively? Yes___No___
3. Do the interactions between us make me feel less attractive and a less enjoyable companion, rather than bolstering my good feelings about myself? Yes___No___

4. Do I feel that I can do little right in my spouse's opinion, or he in mine? Yes___No___
5. Might the negative interactions between us be hurting our children's self-confidence and self-esteem? Yes___No___
6. Has either of us had any serious accidents that might be attributable to the distraction and depression that comes from our poor relationship? Yes___No___
7. Does anyone in our family suffer from physical problems that are linked to stress (see pages 56 and 57)? Is it possible that marital discord is contributing to making one of us sick? Yes___No___

Part Two

Myths about Divorce

How Bias Shapes Your Thinking

Step 6: Take an inventory—What are my fears about separating and divorcing? What stigma and shame do I fear from my family, friends, religion, and community?

If you are unable to think clearly because of anxiety, but continue to fear the consequences of separation and divorce, let's try to put your fears in some perspective. Part of what is clouding your thinking are attitudes and beliefs you have already formed about divorce as a result of living in our society. You may be surprised to learn that some of your anxiety is exaggerated, and is rooted in the distortions about divorce created by biased research published in the popular media.

Research Can Support Both Sides

You can find articles and studies by eminent government-funded researchers about divorce that show almost anything you want to find: higher rates of earlier death, increased mental and physical illness, higher bankruptcy rates, and higher juvenile delinquency and school dropout rates among children of the divorced. You can also find articles and studies by other eminent government-funded researchers, many of which we describe, which make the exact opposite case—that adults and children from unhappy families are ultimately better off in almost every way after a divorce. The one thing all these conflicting researchers do agree about is that it is very difficult to reliably separate the damaging effects of years of living in an unhappy marriage from the effects of divorce. Ask yourself: *What is the toll my unhappy marriage has already taken on me, my spouse, and our children? Is the situation likely to get better or worse if I remain in the marriage?*

Research about divorce gets incredibly complicated, and is profoundly affected by which divorced families you study, and when in the cycle of separation and divorce you study them. If you ask separated women whether their kids' fathers are involved with the children, you will get different answers than if you ask the fathers of those children how involved they are. Who is telling the truth? Most studies just ask mothers, so we only get their point of view.

If you ask separated women whether their kids' fathers are involved with the children, you will get different answers than if you ask the fathers of those children how involved they are. Who is telling the truth? Most studies just ask mothers, so we only get their point of view.

Mary M. Nofsinger points this out in the Introduction to her comprehensive book on the divorce literature, *Children and Adjustment to Divorce: An Annotated Bibliography*. Professor Nofsinger works at the Washington State University Libraries. For this book, she reviewed more than six hundred studies on divorce as it affects parents and children. She introduces the book with a warning: "Often data [from studies of divorce] is collected from clinical populations who are the most adversely affected by divorce. . . . To put it bluntly, clinical studies generally focus on problems and failures to cope rather than on successes and coping abilities."

If you interview people six months to one year after they separate, you catch them at the time of greatest disruption to their lives. Interview them again three years later and you get quite a different, and a much more favorable, report.

For example, Census data reveal that poor people and minorities divorce in greater numbers than do the middle class. Poor people and minorities suffer greater physical, mental, and economic hardship than everyone else in the society because they get worse health care, poor employment and housing opportunities, and are still widely discriminated against. These harsh and unfair societal disadvantages also frequently lead to worse outcomes for poor or minority adults and children who divorce. The hardships suffered by these groups lead to more stress in their lives, which leads to more divorce and to poorer outcomes after divorce. The divorce statistics too often report this as a problem of divorce rather than a problem of poverty and discrimination.

Media Bias

Granted, divorce is difficult under the best of circumstances, but the media—including television, magazines, newspapers, blogs, and Web sites—too frequently present a one-sided view in telling the story about divorce, and make an already difficult situation seem much worse. They encourage us to believe in many myths about the negative impact of divorce, such as damage to women's financial situations and to children's well-being. An exception is the media's double standard when it comes to divorce among celebrities. Here the media seems to glamorize and sensationalize divorce.

Research done by McGill University media studies graduate student J. A. Chevalier, written up in an unpublished dissertation, illustrates this common media bias clearly. She looked at seventy-five articles and stories that appeared in the mainstream media, and found that seventy-two of them reflected a one-sided negative bias against all things divorce-related. The old adage in the media business is "If it bleeds, it leads." It's not news if the lead reads: "Audrey Jones's divorce has gone smoothly and she, her children, and her former spouse are all doing well in their new lives." Gory and heart-rending stories about the suffering and ruin caused by divorce sell magazines, even though these kinds of events are relatively rare. It is inevitable that this extreme and systematic distortion shapes all of our perceptions.

One recent example is an article titled "Divorce, Unwed Parents May Cost Billions," written by David Crary and published by *Nation News*. According to the article, research shows that divorce and out-of-wedlock childbirths cost U.S. taxpayers more than $112 billion annually for social services like welfare. Critics of the study point out that lumping divorced women together with out-of-wedlock mothers is completely inaccurate. It is true that 40 percent of American children are born to single mothers, mostly teenage women who have never been married. A disproportionate number of these women live below the poverty line. Their children's fathers are frequently men who have limited education, have never worked, or who have been imprisoned, thus vastly limiting their earning potential. This is a serious and costly problem in our society, but it is not one that has anything to do with divorce. This article is an example of media bias, a popular publication picking up a story and uncritically reporting it as a "divorce" story.

Poverty and Discrimination

Vanessa, a fifty-year-old African-American woman, told us she grew up in extreme poverty in the rural South. She has earned her living in a combination of legitimate businesses, and has augmented her income by taking bets on daily numbers, an illegal activity. Vanessa raised her children alone in the inner city after their father abandoned the family, and she subsequently divorced him. Two of her children developed drug problems in adolescence, but in adulthood they are drug-free, married, in stable families, and employed. One child is in prison. One met an untimely tragic death. Even though Vanessa and her family have suffered greatly in their lives and she is divorced, theirs is hardly a story of the damaging effects of divorce. It is a story about the effects of growing up in extreme poverty and suffering racial discrimination, conditions in which bad things are likely to happen, especially to minority boys. Today Vanessa is remarried. She and her husband have an antiques business in a rural area.

To lump severely economically disadvantaged populations with broader divorce statistics is an error. It's a misrepresentation to attribute to divorce the damage to adults' and children's lives when they are born into extreme poverty and suffer educational, housing, and employment discrimination. That may be convenient, but it is false.

Don't Be Falsely Influenced

The power of media bias to affect our thinking about divorce is beautifully illustrated in Stephanie Coontz's study, conducted at the University of Virginia. She had two groups of teachers watch the same videotape of an active and curious young child in a classroom. The first group of teachers was told that the child was from a divorced family. The second group was not told anything about the child's family, but watched the same tape. The teachers who were told that the child was from a divorced family saw many problems in the child's behavior. The group of teachers who were not told anything about the child's family saw few or no behavioral problems and described this same child as perfectly normal, active, and curious.

When you think about separation and divorce, you conjure up all the negative stereotypes of divorced families that you have formed, and that makes it difficult to see your situation clearly.

If separating and divorcing had such terrible consequences as the mainstream media would have us believe, why would the overwhelming majority of adults and their children feel better off about their situation several years after the adults end their unhappy marriage? Keep in mind the statistics we opened this book with.

- Psychologist Judith Wallerstein has studied the same sixty divorced families and their children for more than twenty-five years. Even though she is known for her emphasis on the negative consequences of divorce on adults and children, she reports in her book *Second Chances* that five years after divorce 75 percent of women feel better off, and have recovered financially, whether they initiated the divorce or not.
- Wallerstein and others contend that five years after divorce, two-thirds of men report strong preferences for their postdivorce lives, improved incomes, new and better relationships with women, and, in many cases, improved relationships with their children.
- In their book *Divided Families,* leading American sociologists Frank Furstenberg and Andrew Cherlin reported on their study of more than fifteen thousand children from divorced families. They found that two years after their parents' separation or divorce, over two-thirds had stayed the same or improved in their schoolwork and behavior, compared with their performance prior to their parents' ending their unhappy marriage.

You experience that your marriage isn't working well for you. But what fears prevent you from being able to clearly think through your situation, or even to talk about it with a counselor or a lawyer? The following are many of the common myths that the bias against divorce leads most of us to believe. We pose them, debunk them, and attach our "Truth Barometer" to each one. While some of them are "Completely and Absolutely False," and others are "Mostly False" or "Partially True," none are entirely "True."

Divorce Myth #1: We're just going through a rough patch. If I hang in there, things will get better in time.

Truth Barometer Rating: Partially True

Sometimes things do get better. Some things are time-related. The tension at work may pass. Your elderly sick mother who demands so much time and energy either will get better or, God forbid, pass away. Your young child will start school, and you'll have a breather. Researchers have found again and again that the birth of a baby and the raising of a very young child impose one of the greatest strains on a marriage.

Some things can get better with your active intervention, commitment, and persistence. If your spouse drinks or gambles too much, and you can get him or her to commit to a program of change and accept your support, yes, things may get better. If your spouse habitually flirts with other women, you might be able to make him understand that this upsets you and get him to stop.

Some things you can't get any control over, such as her refusal to stop drinking to excess, or his brushing off the hurt you feel when he flirts with other women with the excuse that he's just a "male nymphomaniac" and that's why you were attracted to him in the first place. Decide—can you live with this? If not, be proactive, try to change it, but also, put a time limit on it. You don't want to wait a lifetime for some of these things to change, and then realize when it's too late that they never will.

Divorce Myth #2: If I were really ready to end it, I'd feel certain. I'd know for sure, and I wouldn't have such mixed feelings, as I do now.

Truth Barometer Rating: Completely and Absolutely False

It would be easier to make the decision to divorce if your mate really did something utterly dreadful—if she were Lizzie Borden, the axe murderer. But that's not likely to happen. Most marriages are unhappy in ways that aren't very spectacular. You are bound to feel ambivalent about ending even a terrible marriage. You started the marriage with hope and expectation. You saw positive traits in your spouse. Some of these still remain. Getting out of a marriage requires a lot of effort and a willingness to change. It's scary. It would be very unusual if you didn't have mixed feelings. You don't have a crystal ball. You only know the present, and you can't see into the future. All you can do is accept that you are likely to have these mixed feelings no matter which decision you make, whether you try to work it out or divorce.

Decide how many years you will let yourself think about—and talk yourself out of—divorce.

If you're constantly thinking about divorce, something is seriously wrong in the marriage, and you need to do something to repair it or end it. Most people feel their marriage was dead for years before they got the courage to announce the funeral.

Divorce Myth #3: I will be alone. I will never find another mate.

Truth Barometer Rating: Mostly False

Seventy-five percent of women and 83 percent of men remarry after they divorce, according to the American Institute of Matrimonial Attorneys. This doesn't even include people who have "significant others," but do not remarry. So the odds that you will remain alone, if you do not want to, are small.

Divorce Myth #4: I will be alone. My family, friends, and religious community will reject me.

Truth Barometer Rating: Mostly False

While some religions formally prohibit divorce, a few even to this day cast out and shun divorced (or widowed or elderly) women. The basis for the myth that you will be rejected by your community if you divorce is, in part, a remnant of old traditions. For the most part, our modern cultures thankfully no longer subscribe to these cruel treatments, and even offer ways to dissolve marriages usually without having to withdraw from your religious community.

We asked clergy of different faiths who are educators and pastoral leaders in their religious communities to comment on how their congregations and religious communities respond to separating and divorcing men, women, and children.

Reverend Elizabeth R. Goodman says:

> As the pastor of the Monterey United Church of Christ (located in rural Massachusetts), I don't take a stand on divorce per se, and neither does my denomination. I recognize that marriages are complex, people are complicated and life is sometimes very confusing, so divorce is, on occasion, a necessity. It's something I grieve about more than judge.

Kip Banks, pastor of East Washington Heights Baptist Church in Washington, D.C., had this to say about his experience of divorce in his church:

> My observation after serving as pastor of an African-American Baptist Church for more than seven years is that on the issues of divorce and separation our church community tends to be distant and uninvolved.

> I have seen several couples go through separation and divorce, but the church community just tends to accept it with resignation. There isn't too much stigma attached to divorce in the African-American church and there is also a hesitance among church members to get involved in other people's marriage relationships. The couples going through separation and divorce tend to be embraced in the same manner that they were before the breakup, but this is not good because divorce can be a very traumatic experience.
>
> To address the issues of separation and divorce, our church offers marital counseling, but again it can be difficult to get members to avail themselves of this resource. Sometimes there seems to be more stigma attached to getting marital counseling than getting an actual divorce. Our church is working to establish a comprehensive marriage ministry, including mentor couples who can act as an additional resource for hurting marriages.

Rabbi Andrew Davids of the Hebrew Union College–Jewish Institute of Religion, a nationally recognized expert on Jewish communal leadership, told us:

> Divorced [Jewish] adults are not shunned and they and their children are welcomed as full participants in communal life; however, little work is done on the part of the community to offer alternate models of adult lives and families that reflect the reality of divorced life.
>
> I am certain that this lack of attention has a spiritual impact on individuals experiencing divorce and separation who are looking to Judaism for support during a time of challenging transition. As individuals begin the process of dismantling their marriage, they need more robust and proactive responses that state unequivocally that they remain valued members of the community. In the aftermath of a separation and divorce, the comforting embrace of the community must be extended to these individuals, who are looking for meaning during this new stage in their lives.

We heard the following from James F. Linzey, doctor of divinity, who is a chaplain with the rank of major in the U.S. Army and who has served in Operation Iraqi Freedom. Chaplain Linzey is currently attached to the Walter Reed Army Hospital in Bethesda, Maryland.

Do not to hide what is going on out of shame. Whether or not you initiate the divorce, it's important to lay the groundwork with family, friends, and your religious community (if you enjoy an open and close relationship)—and even help your employer understand your actions—as soon as possible. We call this "getting your side of the story out."

Over half of the warriors who come to me for counseling are about to go through divorce or have been divorced once or twice. It's one of the most common problems I deal with. It's the same old story with many military personnel, and a given, that they have experienced divorce or will experience it. Numerous older warriors who have served in active combat reminisce that after two or three marriages they have finally figured out what they were doing wrong. The disappointment in failed marriages contributes to a casual attitude toward divorce and remarriage in the military. Consequently, there is empathy but no surprise among military members when a divorce occurs. The perception in the military is generally the same as in American society. Divorce is seen as unfortunate, but not more than that.

When a divorce occurs on a military base in the States, the more involved the military couple or family have been in base activities, the sadder the consequences are. Relationships with military couples, families, and children in close association to the divorcing couple and their children, are often broken. A base is a tight-knit community.

Discrimination against both male and female divorcees has decreased considerably since the enormous increase in divorce beginning in the 1970s. Even so, it is important to manage your public image in your community, at work, and in your extended family if you are separating. One of the reasons we include advice on preparing a plan in the last chapter—should you decide it's time to go—is to protect you from people rushing to judgment of you. If other people don't see obvious signs of your separation coming, or fail to understand the reasons for your breakup, it can be hard at first for them to adjust to your new situation. That doesn't mean they won't eventually come around.

There are likely to be some relationship casualties in a divorce. Oftentimes, people take sides. When Joe left Theresa, most of their friends turned their backs on him and sympathized with her. Reflecting back on the situation, Joe realized that he hadn't told people that he was unhappy with Theresa and thinking of divorce. His relationships were superficial, even with his pastor, so he never confided in anybody. On the other hand, Theresa had been talking about their marital problems for a couple of years. So her family, several of their friends, and even their pastor knew Theresa's side of the story and had become sympathetic, lacking any other point of view from Joe.

Bret got his story out with better results. When he thought about leaving Barbara, he told his parents that he was thinking of separating. He was shocked when they poured out their hearts to him, sharing how sad they had been watching his unhappy married life for twenty years. His colleagues at work, in whom he confided, were also supportive. Bret had thought that many in his family and community would turn their backs on him if he divorced. In reality, when he opened up to them, they weren't surprised. They seemed to be wondering what had taken him so long.

If you have been somewhat of a loner all your life, like Joe, it will be harder to connect with other people, but it may also be less important to you than to someone who needs a lot of support. If you have been more social, like Bret, sharing with others will be easier. If you don't want to be alone, you have a choice. There are many people in your community who are in your situation, and there are lots of different ways to find each other. Divorce support groups are easy to find on the Internet, as are single-parent groups.

If you decide it's time to go, get your side of the story out to the people you care about, and accept that you will need to rebuild your social network.

Divorce Myth #5: Someone else will come along and make my spouse really happy.

Truth Barometer Rating: Partially True

Right now your spouse is not making you happy, and you probably aren't making him happy, either. You each have the potential for marital happiness; you need to decide if you can achieve this happiness in your marriage, or if it's already too late.

Sometimes what's not appealing for one person is attractive to another. Jimmy's wife couldn't stand that he had opinions about everything, even in areas that she considered "her domain," like who she should hire as a secretary in her business, or how she should cook a roast beef. His second wife says she loves how diverse and well-informed Jimmy is, and how freely he shares advice and information with her. Sometimes she takes his suggestions, and other times she feels he is a pain in the neck and ignores him, but overall she enjoys, rather than feels threatened by his active mind.

Bert told us when he tried to speak romantically to his former wife, she'd say, "Stop rhapsodizing." His second wife encourages the same kind of talk.

Irv was embarrassed by Julie's quirky sense of humor. In company with other people he'd remind them that Julie was making one of her "Julie jokes," which Julie took as a put-down. Julie's second husband, Robby, eggs her on when she gets rolling.

Flo's husband Herb was a male chauvinist. He resented her even going out of the house. He was verbally and even sometimes physically abusive, dictatorial, and a womanizer. A few years after they split up, he remarried. Flo was flabbergasted at the new leaf he had apparently turned over when she heard about Herb's new life from mutual friends. According to them, Herb became a dutiful and respectful husband to his second wife, and from all accounts settled into a harmonious and mutually satisfying marriage. While we do not know for certain, it seems in all likelihood, that he got professional help in order to accomplish this. In the absence of professional help, it's unlikely that someone who had been abusive would be able to change his ways with a different partner. Flo and Herb were a terrible combination. Their interaction brought out the worst in each of them. Flo went into her marriage with Herb appearing to be a proud and self-confident person. During the marriage she became a shadow of her former self and was very beaten down in reaction to Herb's continual aggression toward her. A few years after Herb remarried, Flo also remarried. In the intervening years, she had recovered a lot of her former verve with the help of therapy. She had once again become independent and self-confident and she married a man who enjoyed these qualities in her, one with whom she has a relationship of equals.

Yes, someone may come along and make your spouse happier than you make her—but someone may also come along and make you happier than your spouse makes you.

Divorce Myth #6: All the problems in my marriage are my fault.
Truth Barometer Rating: Mostly False
Marital problems are never one person's fault. Every relationship is an interaction. Oftentimes, one marital partner refuses to acknowledge that there is any problem in the marriage at all. This leaves the partner who speaks up responsible for any problems in the marriage, and for fixing them alone, which is almost impossible. This scenario represents a total breakdown in communication between the partners.

Each of you is responsible for making the other reasonably content in your marriage. The only way you can do this is if you know how your spouse is genuinely feeling—not just by his words, as he may not be truthful to avoid hurting your feelings, but by his actions.

Marriage is not a win/lose model; it is a win/win or a lose/lose proposition only.

Rick wanted a new car, but his wife Audrey didn't want to spend the money. From Audrey's point of view, there was a very large tree in their front yard that had died several years before. Audrey wanted it taken down, although this was going to be quite expensive. Rick said he didn't want to spend the money to take the tree down, and besides, he loved the shape of the dead tree; to him it was a piece of sculpture, and he wanted to keep it standing. They were stuck in a win/lose model of relating. They each felt that if one of them were to get their way, the other couldn't. They each used the excuse that they shouldn't spend all that money. They each wanted what they desired, but explicitly did not want the other to have his or her way. Rick and Audrey were in a power struggle with each other. Rick wanted a new car, and, although they had the money, Audrey didn't want him to have it. Audrey wanted to have a big dead tree removed from the front yard; Rick didn't want her to get her way. Separately, these two issues went on for months, with each person intent on stopping the other from getting what they wanted. This is the win/lose model. They told us that they were bickering when a friend suggested combining the two problems into one solution. They should get the new car and cut the tree down. For some reason they could accept this input from their friend. They realized that each could get their way; they didn't have to keep struggling over these issues. They hit on a win/win solution, and they were both satisfied.

Divorce Myth #7: If I divorce, I will need to accept it as a personal failure.

Truth Barometer Rating: Partially True

Marriage is a great commitment, an investment of your optimism, faith, energy, emotion, trust, time, and conviction. Many people resonate with sincerity to the words said in the blessing of marriage: "What God hath wrought, let no man cast asunder." The end of a marriage is indeed a failure to live up to these commitments and this optimism. On the other hand, living in a chronically unhappy marriage is also a failure. It is a failure of honesty with oneself and one's partner. It is an unwillingness to accept the loss and open the possibility of moving forward for the entire family. Many people have told us, "I would be so ashamed to admit how bad my marriage is to my family and my friends; it would be such an admission of defeat."

To the outside world, Chris and Lila have it all. He is a handsome, successful businessman in a glamorous and lucrative business. She is beautiful and the mother of four attractive children. They live in a luxurious house in a gated community in an affluent suburb. Chris, for his part, has convinced himself that their complete lack of intimacy, their frequent fighting, their youngest son's serious troubles in school, academically and behaviorally, and Lila's substantial weight gain and sad and depressed manner are all perfectly normal.

Lila is Chris's psychological prisoner. She knows she is unhappy in the marriage and she blames Chris, who she also suspects is unfaithful to her. She resents that he controls her. He won't allow her to get any help in the house although they are affluent. She is a talented painter who sold her paintings before they were married. She has given up painting because Chris considers it a waste of her time and because they don't need the money. Chris disparages her and puts her down at every turn, including criticizing her parenting, which, other than house cleaning, is the main way she expresses herself.

At Lila's insistence, they came into marriage counseling. After one meeting, Chris withdrew, saying that he didn't feel he needed it; he's content with his life. Lila continued to come on her own. Over the course of about eight months, she genuinely began to change. She took a firm stand with Chris and insisted they hire a housekeeper occasionally so she didn't spend all her time cleaning their large house. She became more consistent with their son, and his behavior and grades starting improving in school. She began painting again, and even made plans to exhibit at a local art gallery.

But then Lila started talking in counseling about how worried she was about Chris's response to the changes she was making. She was losing weight, making herself more attractive, and felt more upbeat. He seemed to resent or fear these changes, and his way of expressing this was to deny that she was making any changes at all. He said she was wasting their money on the therapy. He increased his disparagement of Lila and her so-called "new independence." Chris's message was clear. Lila had two choices: Get back to their old marriage and get rid of this therapist, "or else"—whatever the "or else" meant. Lila experienced this message as a menacing threat, worrying that perhaps there was another woman, or that Chris might consider divorcing her if she didn't tow the line. She began to talk in therapy about how humiliated she would be if her marriage failed. All the people she knew from church would be shocked, since everyone saw Chris as such a catch. After a few of these conversations, she dropped out of counseling, presumably to return to the status quo, to give in to Chris's threats, and to avoid what Lila thought of as failure.

Are we to call her remaining in her marriage a "success"? Lila is only about forty. Which would be the greater failure—for her to end this relationship, which is so destructive to her and at least one of their children, or to remain indefinitely in this seemingly failed and hopeless situation?

Divorce Myth #8: No one has my interests at heart except my spouse. When the chips are down and I'm sick or broke, there won't be anyone else to turn to.

Truth Barometer Rating: Mostly False

Those who subscribe to this way of thinking are not only being ruled by a worst-case scenario, but more important, by the most minimal expectation of what it means for another person to "have your interest at heart." Cynthia told us that, at age fifty, she found out she had breast cancer that required a mastectomy. Her husband, Reggie, dutifully drove her to and from the hospital for surgery, but not for any of the other follow-up treatments she required. He was uninvolved with her physicians and the mountain of paperwork she faced from her insurance company. Worst of all, he failed to provide her with the emotional support she badly needed. Nonetheless, in this life crisis, Cynthia clung to Reggie; she believed that because he was her husband he must have her best interests at heart. After she recovered sufficiently, Reggie left her. During a second bout with cancer several years later, Cynthia, now divorced, depended on her grown son and her close friends for support. She received much more comfort and involvement from all of them than she ever did from Reggie.

When Gordon had prostate cancer, he ran into the same issues. His wife Jill didn't physically abandon him, but was fairly quickly intolerant and critical of the sexual side effects that are so prevalent in the aftermath of prostate surgery. No matter how cold and rejecting she was, Gordon clung to her for dear life. He didn't get much of a life raft.

The way your mate acts with you every day is usually a good indication of how she will act when the chips are down.

When Diane totaled her car and wound up in the hospital, her husband Jeff, establishing that Diane was shaken but not badly injured, finally managed to put aside time from work to visit her in the hospital. Diane told us how she longed to see and be comforted by him, and to feel that he was upset over her terrible accident. She got none of that. Her parents and friends, on the other hand, made themselves available to her physically and emotionally, both in the hospital and during her convalescence at home.

The old saying goes, "You can't get blood from a stone." In the examples above, Reggie, Jill, and Jeff have hearts of stone. We all need more than one person to get us through the tough times. First and foremost, however, make sure you are married to someone who will stand by you and support you when things are difficult.

Divorce Myth #9: I'll make the same mistake again and get into another bad marriage with someone just like my spouse, or worse!

Truth Barometer Rating: Partly True

Almost half of all second marriages wind up in divorce. There are, however, ways to reduce your likelihood of making the same mistake again. The better you understand your contributions to the breakdown of your first marriage, the better equipped you will be to avoid repeating your mistakes if you remarry. To picture yourself as merely the victim of your spouse is a mistake. Failure to take responsibility for your actions, or to see yourself as an active participant in your marriage, will prevent you from improving your situation. No one is entirely a victim; it is important to take responsibility for your part in what is happening, no matter how unpleasant that may seem to you.

After Tom died, Amanda remarked to us, "You know, Tom yelled at me, bossed me around, and hardly ever had a kind word for me in the forty years we were married. I always felt like I was Tom's victim. But the other day I was remembering that he asked me for years, 'Amanda, please put the scissors back in the same drawer in the kitchen that you took them out of,' and I never did. I always put them wherever it was convenient. It was so upsetting to Tom when he couldn't find them." What we suspect is that there were lots of incidents where Amanda was not simply Tom's victim, but where she played a very active role in perpetuating their lifelong marital problems.

After Johannes was divorced from Helene for several years, people began to ask him how he could have married such a cold and unappealing woman. At first he was at a loss for an answer. Eventually, he realized that in order to have married Helene, who he had to admit was not right for him, he had to come to grips with how aimless, lonely, and lacking in self-worth he must have been at the time they got together. Philosophers have said, "A person who doesn't remember their past is destined to repeat it." By remembering and understanding his past, by understanding how unhappy he must have been, Johannes put himself in a better position to avoid making the same mistake again. This freed him not to marry "the same" woman again when he sought a new wife.

Try to understand what you saw in your spouse early on that is turning out to be such a disappointment now. Were you attracted to your mate's good looks or income without thinking enough about his character? Did you find it "cute" or "charming" that he was a bit unreliable, flaky, flirtatious, self-absorbed, took financial risks, gambled or drank heavily, and so forth? All these "devilish" qualities can be quite appealing in the early stages of a relationship, but they wear thin over time. Are you still attracted by these traits? If so, you may want to seek them out in much smaller quantities in your next partner.

If you leave your spouse, you should absolutely not rush into a second marriage. Seeking counseling first can help you to understand yourself sufficiently to avoid acting in haste and "repenting at leisure."

Divorce Myth #10: I'll be ruined financially.

Truth Barometer Rating: Mostly False

In her influential 1985 book, *The Divorce Revolution,* Harvard University professor Lenore Weitzman asserted that after divorce women and children suffer a 73 percent drop in their standards of living, while fathers experience a 42 percent increase. These powerful statistics have shaped an entire generation's laws, social policies, and beliefs about the financial implications of divorce. They are still widely circulated in the media. There is only one problem with them: They are false. After eleven years of denial, Dr. Weitzman publicly acknowledged that her computations were in error.

In 1999 Arizona State University professor Sanford Braver, in his book *Divorced Dads,* reported that men and women fare roughly the same financially following a divorce. Braver demonstrated that, within a couple of years of divorcing, both men and women for the most part maintain or rebound to the same lifestyles they had prior to their divorces. Dr. Braver's study was federally financed, spanned ten years, and followed the lives of four hundred men and women who were divorcing. It was unique in that he mostly interviewed men and women who had recently divorced one another. He asked them about their finances as well as their custody and child-care arrangements.

In fact, according to the U.S. Census Bureau, fewer than 25 percent of women experience any significant drop in income postdivorce. Similar to the results of Dr. Braver's research, the Census confirms that more than half of women who do experience a drop in income recover financially within a few years to approximately their predivorce levels. This is as a result of their gaining or expanding their employment and/or remarrying.

Paying lawyers' fees and supporting two households do represent a financial burden that feels like a terrible hardship, at least temporarily. It isn't as if there is no financial effect caused by divorcing; we will discuss some of this in a later chapter. Long term, however, Braver's research, U.S. Census Bureau data, and almost all our interviews show both men and women returning to their former lifestyle within a few years following divorce.

Studies from the University of Michigan and the U.S. Census Bureau also reveal that the great fear that a woman will be "plunged into poverty" because of divorce is very rarely true. Studies show that people who are living in poverty after they divorce were not "plunged into poverty" because of the separation; they were already living in or on the brink of poverty prior to their divorce. The slightest decrease in their incomes drove them statistically into the "below poverty level" category. In this same vein, the U.S. Census Bureau data reports that for 75 percent of people who descend below the poverty line, lost income—not divorce—is the cause. Once you fall into poverty, however, the likelihood of your having marital problems increases greatly.

One of the single greatest causes of divorce is financial stress brought on by unemployment or dramatically reduced income, due to taking a new job at a much-reduced rate of pay.

Nobel Prize–winning economist Lester Thurow states that it is not divorce that causes poverty, but poverty that causes divorce. He is right. When you lose your job, or are forced to take a much lower-paying job, it puts terrible stress on your marriage and frequently leads to divorce. Men and women who have divorced often describe job loss or reduced family income as having preceded their divorce.

We interviewed Louis, a taxicab driver and American citizen who emigrated from Haiti to the United States thirty years ago as a youngster. Today he lives with his second wife and their two children and owns and drives a taxicab. As he recounts:

> I used to be a mechanic for one of the airlines. After my company went under, I was offered four other jobs with the airlines, but every one of them was for half the money I was making before. My first wife and I couldn't live with the two kids on that. We started fighting and that's when I left. I still see my kids and I give her money for them. I never could get a good job again, so I drive the cab. I'm thinking of moving to Atlanta. I heard there are good jobs there.

Divorce Myth #11: My children will be damaged forever and I will lose control of raising them, or their father will lose interest in them and drop out of all of our lives.

Truth Barometer Rating: Mostly False

By and large, it is conflict and alienation between parents that damages children's (and adults') well-being. If you divorce, you and your spouse should try to settle your financial and parenting issues as quickly and amicably as possible. After a transition period, and once the conflict between the spouses dies down, children in divorced families generally do as well or better in school performance and behavior than children from unhappy families. As we mentioned previously, Frank Furstenberg and Andrew Cherlin's mammoth study of more than fifteen thousand children who had experienced divorce demonstrated this.

As for dads losing contact with their kids as a result of divorce, fathers appear to be getting a bad rap. Contrary to the prevailing belief that around half of fathers lose contact with their children within a few years after a divorce, Sanford Braver's research at Arizona State University further demonstrates that 90 percent of dads continue to have contact with their children at least once a week after divorce. His research shows that, even three years later, five out of six fathers continue to live in the same town as their children.

Unlike many other researchers studying fathers' involvement with their children after divorce, Dr. Braver interviewed both divorced moms and their former husbands, getting both sides of the story. Most other researchers in this area only interview the divorced moms, and therefore only hear their possibly biased or angry view of the contact and level of interest between dads and their children. In Dr. Braver's study, in the 10 percent of cases where the father's contact with the children was erratic or infrequent, it was sometimes the mothers or the courts denying the dads access to their children—sometimes for good reasons, sometimes not.

Researcher Sarah Schoppe-Sullivan of Ohio State University studies fathers' involvement with their children in intact families. She demonstrates that a father's involvement is heavily influenced by the mother's attitude toward it. If the father is strongly encouraged by the mother to be active and involved with his children, not surprisingly, there exists more paternal involvement. However, if the mother is strongly critical or discouraging of paternal participation, fathers become less involved, or in some cases even give up. This is true in both intact and divorced families.

After Richard and his wife separated and started angry divorce proceedings, he told us that he had a lot of trouble gaining access to his son Michael. After he moved out, he took an apartment in the same town, and gained liberal visitation rights in their separation agreement. However, frequently when he would try to make arrangements to see Michael or go to pick him up, Samantha would make one excuse after another as to why Michael was unavailable. Suddenly, Michael could only take religious instruction and piano lessons on the very same days and times that Richard was able to get off from work to see their son. Other times, all Richard could do was act as a chauffeur and drive Michael to soccer practice or the dentist and wait until the activity was over so he could drive Michael directly back to his mother's so the boy could do his homework, as the visitation time was over. Samantha was rigid in adhering to these time schedules, to Richard's great frustration.

The only alternative that Richard had was to take Samantha to court, at considerable expense, time, and bitterness, in order to see his son more conveniently and consistently. The young son was strongly influenced by his mother's negative attitudes toward spending time with his father. For his part, the boy would be temperamental, distant, and negative most of the time when he was with his dad. This discouragement went on for years, putting great strain on Richard, before he and Michael gradually worked out their own better relationship.

During this time, if a researcher had only asked Samantha, she probably would have said that Michael's father saw little of their son. In her anger at Richard, she might even have been tempted to say that he didn't seem to have much interest in Michael at all. This is why Dr. Braver's study, which includes both divorced parents, keeps both parties more truthful and reveals fathers' commitment to continued involvement. Dr. Schoppe-Sullivan's research in 2007 confirms that the mother's attitude (usually she is the custodial parent) is crucial to the successful involvement of the father.

You may be particularly worried if you have heard the myths that divorce is always hardest on boys and young children. In psychologist Abigail Stewart's study of 160 families from Greater Boston, which all included the custodial parent and school-aged children six or older, she found virtually no evidence to support either of these contentions. She did find that when the conflict between parents continued long after the separation, it was hard on both boys and girls, causing boys to have more behavior problems and girls to have more physical symptoms and emotional distress. These symptoms are characteristic of boys and girls in general when they are under stress, not just stress related to the conflict in their parents' marriage or conflict after a separation and divorce.

Divorce Myth #12: My marriage is no different than anyone else's; I have excessive, unreasonable expectations of what a marriage should be.

Truth Barometer Rating: Completely and Absolutely False.

You have the right to expect support, loyalty, respect, and more from your marriage. Reread chapter 2, "The Marriage Bill of Rights."

Questions to Think About

1. Is it possible that I have been waiting too long for this "rough patch" in my marriage to end? Yes___No___
2. Do I stay, in part, because I am afraid that no one else will want me? Yes___No___
3. Do I stay, in part, because I am ashamed to admit to myself, my friends, or my family that my marriage isn't working? Yes___No___
4. Do I stay, in part, because I am afraid that I will just make the same mistakes again if I divorce and eventually remarry? Yes___No___
5. Do I stay, in part, because I am afraid that if I divorce I will be financially ruined? Yes___No___
6. If we separate, can I accept it if my mate finds someone else who makes him happier than I have? Yes___No___
7. Do I stay, in part, because I am afraid my mate will reject or neglect our children if we divorce? Yes___No___

CHAPTER 8

Divorce Versus the Unhappy Marriage

News media and scholarly publications frequently make the error of evaluating the negative effects of divorce on people's lives by comparing them with the lives of people from intact families. Closer scrutiny reveals the faulty logic in this comparison. To assess whether you should end your marriage, you must compare living in a divorced family with its realistic alternative, living in a family that is chronically unhappy, that is in open conflict, or that is hopelessly stalemated and alienated. This comparison leads to a very different understanding of the effects of divorcing or remaining in an unhappy marriage. The group that researchers call "intact families" includes both happy and unhappy families in approximately equal numbers.

What lumping these very different groups together as "intact families" does is to distort what's happening in the unhappy family. It minimizes the negative health consequences, the negative effects on the children, the loss of self-esteem, the reduction of sexual contact, the depression, and all the other negative ramifications we have cited that result from living in an unhappy marriage. Therefore, much of the data on the supposed alternative to divorce—data collected about "intact families"—is inaccurate. The real alternative to divorce for the vast majority of people is continuing to live in an unhappy, intact family, and the statistics that are available, when this comparison is made, generally show better outcomes for most people after they divorce.

The Win/Win Model

Let's take two examples—one of life in a happy marriage and the other of life in an unhappy marriage. When Alex and Leslie moved into their new house, they were full of enthusiasm. It was late spring, the house was freshly painted, and the furniture, carpets and drapes had all been cleaned. It was an exciting new start in a new community. They had a small garden, and the two decided to go to a local nursery and shop for some flowering plants. Alex, who likes to cook, had put a corned beef in a pot with water. He put the pot on a low flame, and left it to simmer on the stove. After planning the garden at the nursery and buying the plants, the two thought of several other stops they needed to make before getting back home. When they pulled up to the house hours later, after a lovely day of shopping, Alex thought he smelled someone barbecuing—until they opened the front door. The entire house was filled with a greasy, gray smoke that the four-pound (1.8kg) corned beef had turned into. Not only did the greasy smoke fill every square inch of the house, but the smell was awful.

How did each of them act? Well, of course, they were both upset, but more importantly, Alex didn't defend and Leslie didn't attack. Alex accepted responsibility for his huge mistake and profusely apologized to Leslie for creating this mess. She insisted that it was just as much her responsibility as his; she also could have remembered that the pot was on the stove. The issue that consumed both of them was what they needed to do together to repair the damage. They got to work and after many weeks of considerable effort and expense, they restored the house. The story became a humorous, although rueful, family legend.

Some years later Leslie, who was under a lot of stress at work at the time, absentmindedly left a pot of eggs boiling on the stove and went to work. Fortunately, Alex happened to come home for lunch that day. Yes, once again, the house was filled with smoke. He remembered the compassion Leslie had shown for him years before with the corned beef incident. Without calling her, he got to work to rectify as much of the damage as he could. He knew how upset she would be with herself, and wanted to minimize the additional stress of this accident rather than pile more stress on to his already overextended wife while she was at work. Compare this win/win model of communication with the win/lose model so common among unhappily married couples.

The Win/Lose Model

Gio took his nine-year-old daughter over to his brother's house one Saturday afternoon so she could play with her cousin of the same age.

The two kids were playing on a backyard swing as the brothers drank coffee on the patio nearby. Gio's daughter fell off the swing and broke her arm. They immediately took her to the hospital to have it set. Gio's wife, Anna, had been out running errands. When she got to the hospital a couple of hours later, their daughter's arm was already in a cast. The little girl was pale and a bit shaken, but otherwise fine. Gio's wife was understandably upset about the accident, but she directed all her anger at Gio, whom she blamed for not supervising their daughter properly.

An unhappy, intact marriage often follows a win/lose model in which the feeling of "us" has broken down. Each of you wants to gain the upper hand to finally, once and for all, prove the other wrong. It's more like a war than a marriage.

For months, long after the arm was healed, Anna repeatedly used the incident to bolster her arguments in other disagreements that she and Gio were having in their unhappy marriage. Whenever she had the chance, she "threw in his face" that he was a poor father, irresponsible, self-involved, and careless. This is the win/lose model of communication that we should try to avoid in our marriages if we want them to be happy.

In the win/win model, a couple see themselves as on the same side, so when adverse events occur, they are happening to "us." The fact that an action of your mate's precipitates the adverse event doesn't make him the "bad guy." In fact, it may make him worthy of your compassion because you know he feels bad about it. In the win/lose model of communication, any adverse event is fresh evidence of your mate's inadequacies and your disappointment in him.

So how do you know if you have a serious problem? Which model of communication does your marriage operate with most of the time? If it's the win/lose, we would say you are probably living in an unhappy marriage. You have to make serious efforts to correct this problem. How does anyone in your family benefit if you and your spouse continue to operate as adversaries? What kind of outside help have you sought? How vigorously have you tried to tell your mate that the model of communication the two of you are engaged in together doesn't work for most things, but most assuredly doesn't work for a marriage?

Questions to Think About

1. Do my spouse and I communicate using the win/lose model? Yes___No___
2. Is one or both of us frequently trying to demonstrate the other's shortcomings, mistakes, and inadequacies? Yes___No___
3. Does one or both of us usually try to gain the upper hand to prove the other wrong in a crisis, rather than see the crisis as happening to "us"? Yes___No___

CHAPTER 9

The Transition Period

Perhaps we have convinced you that it is unhealthy for the whole family to remain in a chronically unhappy marriage. You have determined that yours seems chronically unhappy. But you still have many fears about what you can expect if you decide it is time to go, and you take the huge step to separate. Aren't you about to face a whirlwind if you make this decision?

As we noted earlier, popular writers and even many researchers of divorce frequently interview or collect data about recently separated or divorced people. This prevents us from distinguishing between the transitional period of disruption following a divorce and the longer-term, more positive effects that divorce has on many adults and children who were living in unhappy families. People struggling with a troubled marriage are likely to be alarmed if the only images of divorced or separated people they encounter are those in the transitional turmoil of the first year or two after separation. Yet this is usually what is written about in the stories about divorce that appear in the media. Think about it: Most of us know people who have had smooth experiences as well as people who have had turbulent ones. The uneventful divorces aren't much of a story, so they don't get mentioned, but they happen all the time. You may know people casually who are getting married for the second or third time and this is the first time you realize that they had divorced at some time in the past. But even though you know them somewhat, you aren't aware they have gone through a divorce, because their divorce was not particularly acrimonious, and they must not have felt the need to share the details with others outside their very close circle of family and friends.

According to Abigail Stewart in *Separating Together*, the vast majority of divorcing people come to mutually agreed on solutions with a minimum of conflict. Typically, women take around two years and men around one to three years to work through the transition period. While we don't minimize how long this turmoil may seem when we are in the midst of it, we encourage people to take a longer view. For the vast majority of people, life settles down and improves after the transition period; for many, it improves much more quickly.

The positive effects of divorce are usually not fully evident for a few years after separation. Even Judith Wallerstein, well known for her emphasis on long-term damage caused by divorce, supports this fact by pointing out that five or more years after separation, four out of five women feel they are better off divorced than they were in their unhappy marriages, and that the same holds true for an almost equal percentage of children and men.

A Divorcing Family, in the Short Term and Long Term

Donald and his wife Sonia had recently divorced. When Donald and Sonia split up, most of their friends sympathized with Sonia, making Donald into the bad guy and Sonia into the victim—a simplistic and inaccurate judgment. Donald's family—his parents and brother, in particular—openly blamed Donald for the divorce and were upset with him for several years, just when he needed them most. He couldn't speak with them or his friends about his situation, and felt very isolated. At the time of their separation, Donald and Sonia's daughter Abbey, who was eight, became anxious and school-phobic. The girl repeatedly had to be picked up and taken home from school. She experienced these problems for a couple of years, and had similar issues when attempting to sleep over at friends' or relatives' homes.

Donald and Sonia suffered terrible guilt about their daughter's problems. Donald felt that he had made his life a mess, and he went into therapy. As things calmed down between her parents, Abbey's symptoms receded, and she made a normal adjustment to her changed circumstances. Now, sixteen years later, at age twenty-four, Abbey is by all accounts doing well in work and in love. She enjoys warm and loving relationships with both her parents. Donald has rebuilt his life. He is in a satisfying relationship with a woman and in a flourishing career. He has reunited with his siblings. Sonia has remarried.

Earlier, we asked you to evaluate how your marriage is affecting your life, as well as the lives of your spouse and children. In this section, we have asked you to evaluate what you are afraid of in contemplating divorce: the stigma attached to divorce, the fear of being alone, financial fears, fears of loss of reputation and community, and more. We have helped you to sort out myth from reality by educating you on the distortions common in the mainstream media that drive our commonly held perceptions about divorce.

Living in an unhappy family is toxic and cumulative. The longer you stay, the more you pay.

As the old saying goes, there is no such thing as a free lunch. Separation and divorce are a trade-off. What gets torn down, must be rebuilt. Unfortunately, for many of us who've been through it, this process isn't as easy or as fast as we would like.

Questions to Think About

1. When I think about separating, am I unable to take a long-term view, but focus primarily on the disruption I'll face in the short term? Yes___No___
2. Am I aware of the cumulative effects that our unhappy marriage are having on me and the rest of our family, and that the longer I stay, the more we all feel them? Yes___No___

Part Three

Truths about Divorce

Divorce for the Sake of the Children

Step 7: Evaluate realistically—If I divorce, what do I fear will happen to my children? Will I lose them? Can I accept not seeing them every day?

In Part Three: Truths About Divorce, we'll look at what you can expect if you make the decision that it's time to go. We will discuss both the positive and the negative consequences of separating and divorcing. What may the real repercussions likely be for your children—no matter what their ages? What may the real consequences be for you and your spouse, in terms of your finances, your self-esteem, and your relationships?

The Things You Worry About

A prime reason people stay in dead marriages is fear of what will happen to their children. Keeping a marriage together for the sake of the children is the conventional wisdom. Parents of younger children ask themselves these questions:

- *What will happen to my children's academic performance?*
- *How will their behavior be affected in and out of school?*
- *How will our divorcing affect our children's self-esteem?*
- *How will the loss of everyday contact with one of their parents affect them?*
- *How will they feel if they have to move from their home?*
- *Will they lose their friends?*
- *Will they suffer from living at a reduced financial level?*

Parents of adolescent children ask themselves questions like these:

- *How will my teenagers' academic performance and behavior be affected?*
- *How will my children be affected in their social and sexual lives?*
- *Will they get involved with drugs?*
- *Will they start hanging out with a bad crowd?*
- *If I divorce, will it hurt their chances to form happy and lasting marriages someday?*

Children in unhappy, intact families are more likely to have behavior, academic, and self-esteem problems than those from happy or even divorced families.

How can you know if it is better or worse for your children to keep your marriage together or to divorce? In other words, when is it better to divorce for the sake of the children?

Virtually every researcher on the subject agrees that chronic exposure to conflict and/or disrespect—open or covert—is damaging to children, whether the conflict is between the parents or between parent and child.

Keep in mind that it is unrealistic to compare children from divorced families with those from happy, intact families. This is not your likely alternative; happy families do not contemplate divorce.

What is key is the amount of disagreement and disrespect between parents—open or covert—to which children are exposed. While separation and divorce often increase disagreements during the first year or so, it makes sense that in the long run divorce decreases conflict. Exposure to ongoing conflict and disrespect are the main factors that determine the severity of children's problems in and out of school. There are many studies that confirm this, but most especially the lifelong work of professor Mavis Hetherington at the University of Virginia, whom we mentioned earlier. In the same vein, two other researchers, Lee Ann Kot and Holly Shoemaker, working at Syracuse University in 1999, examined the developmental effects of parental conflict on four age groups: infants/toddlers, young children, adolescents, and young adults. They reviewed numerous previously published studies. They found overwhelming evidence that parental conflict—not whether a marriage was intact, or the couple were separated or divorced—was the key factor working against children's positive adjustment.

Children's Behavior and School Performance

If you are the parent of school-aged children and you are weighing your alternatives, it is important to know that after a period of transition most children from divorced families generally do as well or even better in school, both academically and behaviorally, as children from unhappy, intact families. Hetherington, in her massive study of thousands of children from divorced families, found that "two to three years after divorce, children who live in [divorced, mother-headed] one-parent households are doing better, with half as many behavior problems, than children in [unhappy] intact families."

Frank Furstenburg and Andrew Cherlin's research involved fifteen thousand boys, aged seven to eleven. Those from divorced families scored no different in reading or math than children from intact families—happy or unhappy. On measures of behavior and emotional well-being, there was also no difference in these children from divorced families when compared with children from intact families—again, happy or unhappy.

Becoming Normal Again

If you look at your child's behavior or school performance in the year or two after a separation, it may be worse, not better, because the conflict of the marriage often carries over into the early period of separation. In addition, there are new strains brought on by the transition to new living arrangements.

We interviewed a couple, each of them parents, who had met one another and started dating during their respective separations. They described how difficult and chaotic, unpredictable and conflict-filled that period was for each of them and their respective children, two of whom were not doing well in school. This was in 2001. They told us they'd reassured each other, and brought humor into their situation by adopting a slogan, "Normalcy in '03!" Six months into 2003, the phrase became "Normalcy in '04!" They knew at some point that things would settle down. Life did, but it took longer than their original, overly optimistic projections.

When a separation occurs, life is turned upside down for children. They seldom see their parents' separation coming. At first, things often get worse. The household is split apart; for a period of time, conflict may escalate and stability disappears. The children may be unsure where they are sleeping at night; their furniture may be gone; their mother is crying while their father is depressed or sullen; their parents hold closed-door conferences from which they're excluded; there is anxiety about money. These children's lives are destabilized. Much of the security that they had counted on vanishes. This is one of the primary things that people fear about divorce, and it is real but temporary.

The desire to return to "normal" life is one of divorced children's greatest yearnings. What do they mean by *normal*? Are they saying that they want to live with their two parents again? Yes, but we don't think it's that simple. What we found is that there is no single definition of *normalcy*. The concept keeps changing, depending on where they are in the cycle—original unhappy family, separation, divorce, or reestablishment of a new life.

During the years in the unhappy family, prior to separation, many children simply refuse to admit how unhappy they are and how bad their home situation is. They get used to the day-to-day unhappiness and conflict. They find small moments of happiness that they cling to so that they can tell themselves, "Things are normal." They call the stability of their family "normal." This helps them to ignore the conflict. We can hear this denial in the propaganda that members of unhappy families tell each other and the outside world: "Every family has its arguments" or "We fight a lot, but we really love each other." While there is some truth in these statements, in the unhappy, intact family, they also mask serious problems and unsalvageable relationships.

After the transition period, the children's yearnings change. If they could articulate their feelings, this is what we think they would say: "Yes, I wish my parents could have had a happy life with each other, but that can't be, and it's probably best that they broke up. What I really want now is for my parents not to be fighting with each other anymore. I want them each to be happy, and I'd like to have a peaceful, happy home with each of them." That's what you need to aim for, should you decide that it's time to go.

If you decide to separate, especially if your children will live primarily with you, you will need to provide as much continuity for them as you can. Plan to maintain routines, continue to live in the same neighborhood, if you can, so they may attend the same school and keep the same friends to the greatest extent possible. Make sure they see extended family on both your ex-spouse's side and your own as often as they can.

If you separate, you can provide great comfort to your children by reassuring them that things will be all right, that both their mom and dad will provide them with good and loving homes, and that the arguing will diminish. When interviewed during the transition period, most children have told us that they would do anything to return to their original intact family—despite the constant unhappiness and arguing that had gone on. This desire on your children's part for the status quo—even an untenable status quo—may make them resentful and difficult to manage; they may sometimes act sullen, angry, and withdrawn. They need you more than ever during this major transition, although they may do everything in their power to make your being supportive of them difficult and your life miserable in the process.

Children sometimes blame themselves for their parents' breakup. When there is a separation, both parents must repeatedly reassure the children that they did not cause the divorce; the parents divorced for their own reasons, even if their arguments involved the children.

Children's Rejection

A child does not have the scope in his thinking to see the bigger picture; he will be against your separating, no matter how bad things are in your home. This is an extremely difficult decision, even for an adult, and it's part of the reason why you will almost always have some mixed feelings about deciding to divorce.

In considering whether it is time to go, you will need to prepare yourself for the possibility of some temporary coldness from your child, especially if the child blames you for the breakup. But remember, your decision is way too important to allow your child to make it for you.

So, if you fear your child rejecting you, don't panic and convince yourself that this will be a permanent state of affairs; it rarely is. You will need to ward off your own anger toward a child who is distant or disrespectful to you. If you are the noncustodial parent, you will need to be patient and keep the lines of communication open, but possibly make your visits together short and not quite as frequent as you may want. In the beginning, many children tolerate shorter and less frequent visits better than the more frequent visitation to which a parent may be legally entitled. A child has an inherent desire for both of his parents, and will eventually come around without your forcing him to spend more time with you. Let the child slowly come back to you. This takes patience as well as courage, but we have seen it work again and again.

It is likely that after a period of time, your child will reverse her opinion and blame the other parent or cease to blame anyone. If the child starts off blaming the other parent and you are the favored one, you'll need to resist the temptation to agree with the child and reinforce that distance, which will cause your child to become alienated from the other parent. The best approach is to keep reinforcing for your child that this is between Mom and Dad, and both parents, even if they are acting badly at present, love and mean well for the child. Ongoing conflict after separation exacerbates the negative effects already experienced by your children.

Regardless of how you anticipate your child responding, you should be proactive about staying in the picture without forcing the matter. If you are the noncustodial parent, usually the father, decide that you won't drop out of your children's school life. You'll want to alert the school to your new address and ask for your own copy of your children's report cards. If you are not used to being involved, now is the time to play an active role. Show up for Open School Night; even though your ex-spouse will be there, too. Ask your children about school. Remember their friends' names. Show up at Little League games and the school play. You will feel better. You will do better. Research proves that noncustodial parents who stay actively involved with their children's day-to-day lives after separating fare better in many ways, including in their self-esteem and adjustment to single life.

Questions to Think About

1. Are our children growing up in an unhappy, intact family? Yes___No___
2. Are our children frequently exposed to ongoing conflict between my spouse and me? Yes___No___
3. Am I afraid to separate, in part, because I fear our children's anger and possible rejection? Yes___No___
4. Am I afraid that if I am the noncustodial parent I will lose touch with my children's daily lives? Yes___No___

CHAPTER 11

Children's Self-Esteem

Popular wisdom tells us that kids from divorced families have a poorer self-image than children from intact families. As in so many divorce-related areas, the research does not support this. Contrary to what parents worry about, researchers tell us that children's self-esteem is not negatively affected by their parents' divorce. In a review of thirty-seven different studies of children aged three to eighteen, Professor Lorna McKee, at the University of Aberdeen, Scotland, concluded that: "No emotional or behavior problems, or loss of self-esteem, could be demonstrated [in children] because their parents had divorced." For most of us, this is astonishing. We have grown to maturity telling one another that divorce damages children's feelings about themselves. The evidence about the last couple of generations of children flies in the face of this conventional thinking. It is the family conflict before a separation that injures children's self-esteem, not divorce itself.

You and your mate do influence much of your child's self-esteem. Children's self-esteem is heavily dependent on three factors:

1. How much conflict there is between their parents.
2. How much interest their parents take in the children.
3. The income level of their family, in comparison to their friends' and relatives' families.

This puts most kids from lower-income families at a psychological disadvantage when compared with their more affluent peers. Poor behavior and academic performance in children with normal intelligence are linked to the level of conflict, open or under the surface, between a child's parents or between a parent and child. Divorce removes children from day-to-day exposure to conflict between parents and eventually allows the children to recover. Face it: The conflict or alienation between you and your spouse is not just about the two of you. Daily it takes a toll on your children's self-esteem.

Even if it infuriates you that your child's other parent has different rules, or no rules, accept that this is her right as a parent—except in the rare situation when she is putting the child in danger, physically or psychologically.

Not Your Ex But Your Child's Father

If you decide to separate, perhaps the hardest thing you will have to do is also the most important. You will have to stop thinking of your former spouse as your enemy. He may make this extremely hard. From day 1 of a separation, you will need to speak of your ex as your child's father or mother. This approach acknowledges that your child needs his other parent, even if you don't. This may not seem apparent right now. You may be deciding that it's time to go, but both of your roles as parents need to endure. You may disagree on parenting decisions; in fact, that may well be one of the reasons your marriage is falling apart.

Neither of you should undermine, sabotage, or prevent your child from spending time with his other parent, except if this involves genuine danger to the child. Then you should take immediate action. Discuss the problem with your ex-spouse or, if necessary, seek legal counsel to address it. No matter how possessive you feel, you will need to encourage your children's relationship with their other parent. Don't be surprised when they come back after a visit and get easily upset. This is common and occurs because the differences in environment and rules may take some time for them to adjust to—but they will.

Resist Retaliation

If you have made the decision to separate, don't let yourself get drawn back into the relationship; this will only confuse your children further. Have as little to do with your former spouse as possible, except with regard to matters relating to your children, and then try to keep discussions brief and to the point.

If your child blames you for the breakup and acts angrily toward you, you may be tempted to speak badly of the other parent in order to defend yourself. You may be tempted to accuse your child of favoritism.

Don't use your child's poor behavior as an opportunity to criticize the other parent. No matter how hard your former spouse tries to engage you in arguments, try not to take the bait.

You may even feel as if your child is being just like her other parent, the one you are rejecting or who is rejecting you. Please resist the urge to retaliate, bad-mouth, or blame your former spouse to your child, even if it's to defend yourself. We sympathize with you. Your child's behavior is painful, but it is also perfectly normal as she tries to make sense of what has happened to her and her family. Remember that you have been thinking about this decision for a long time, but your children are just starting to catch up with your decision.

From Nightmare to Recovery

Holden's parents' marriage and divorce took a terrible toll on him because the conflict between his parents just kept escalating. His father, Bruce, a forty-two-year-old retailer, owns two sporting goods shops. He was very open in telling us the family's story. Holden's mom is a professional musician who is on call with various local orchestras. The father and mother separated when Holden was eight years old. That was seven years ago. Here is a look at the progression of Holden's behavior and self-esteem through the various stages of marriage and divorce.

The Unhappy Marriage

Bruce described the marriage. He and his former wife are both strong-willed and were locked in an ongoing power struggle throughout their marriage. They each had different but equally rigid views about the roles men and women should play in parenting, work, and socializing. Bruce admits that he was often aloof and angry, and Holden's mother was sometimes depressed and undependable. They argued openly, sometimes escalating into verbal, and on occasion, minor physical abuse of one another. As the child, Holden was frequently put in the position of having to choose sides between them; typically he sided with his mother. She alternated between indulging Holden and rejecting or criticizing him. Because his parents agreed on so little, they were able to place few limits on him. One parent was often undermining the other, and, as a result, Holden's behavior deteriorated. As early as three or four years old, Holden was already caught in the conflict between his parents.

Bruce further explained that at five years old Holden was asked not to return to the preschool he attended. He bullied other children, was uncooperative with teachers, and had to constantly be the center of attention. His preschool teachers called Holden's behavior to his parents' attention, but Bruce and his wife did not take these concerns seriously. We see that Holden's behavior had already become a mirror of his parents' unhappy marriage. The situation worsened until Holden was eight, at which time his mother took the boy and left Bruce.

What gave Holden's mother the courage to leave Bruce? The distance between her and Bruce had been growing for years, as had their conflict over how to deal with Holden. In her case, as frequently happens, particular events appear to have pushed her toward her decision. Bruce's business partnership in his two stores broke up, leading to a subsequent lawsuit. This threatened the family income and the family's comfortable lifestyle. It made her even more dissatisfied with Bruce. A few months later, her mother died suddenly in a tragic automobile accident. Her dad had been deceased for several years, so she was suddenly orphaned. As an only child, she felt more alone than ever, with no parental support. This exaggerated her isolation in her marriage. As was typical of him, Bruce did not respond to her grief. After yet another major argument with Bruce, she realized that she was through. She announced her intention and moved out with Holden a few weeks later. A fierce and protracted legal struggle ensued over custody and the couple's little remaining property.

A Difficult Transition

According to Bruce, when Holden lived with his mother the boy rapidly came to dominate her. This made her so frustrated and alarmed that she escalated her criticism of Holden. Her inability to control him precipitated a crisis in which Holden ran away from home. As a result, Holden went to live with his father, who seemed to be a firmer parent, although he was sometimes heavy-handed in his treatment of Holden. Despite recommendations from Holden's school, his parents made the mistake of not seeking professional help for themselves, and for their parenting of Holden at this point.

You may need professional counseling to help you manage the difficult situations that may arise for you and your children in a separation or divorce.

According to Bruce, once they were separated,

Holden's mother grew more erratic in her parenting responsibilities. She promised to make a birthday party for Holden and then canceled it the day before the event. On days Holden was staying with her, she sometimes wouldn't be home when he came home from school; he'd find a note that she'd be back later because she was rehearsing for a concert.

We can surmise that Holden's domination of his mother mimicked his father's behavior; in addition, it was almost certainly a response to what he experienced as his mother's erratic behavior. He felt encouraged to dominate his mother because he saw her as weak and not competent to manage him. Bruce recalls that at nine years old his son would charm adult acquaintances with pseudosophisticated, adultlike conversation. Holden had strong opinions on everything, even religion and politics. In this light, we can see how Holden's behavior made sense to him. It was his attempt to respond to the chaotic circumstances that he had to live with.

In the year-and-a-half transition period after his parents separated, things got worse for Holden. His parents were in an all-out war against each other, escalating the level of conflict that already had been destroying the marriage. Holden got into trouble in summer day camp. He started out uncooperative and wound up fighting with and hurting other boys on two different occasions. At home with either of his parents, he cursed them and frightened them by running away. The public school, where he was a fourth-grader, was frequently forced to contact the parents. They even brought up the possibility of placing him in a school for disturbed children.

Recovering and Moving On

This crisis proved a turning point in his parents' relationship, with him, and with each other. Bruce noted that conflict levels began to decline. The parents each hired new, less adversarial attorneys. The parents began meeting with a psychologist, who helped them work more cooperatively in their dealings with Holden. This tremendous decrease in the postmarital conflict enabled Holden to start recovering.

The following school year was more successful for Holden. His behavior was within more acceptable limits, although still problematic at times. He made some friends and participated in some school activities. He decreased the level of his confrontational behavior with both his father and his mother. The summer of his eleventh birthday, he had a successful summer at a sleepaway camp.

Over the past few years, there has been a gradual but steady improvement in Holden's functioning in every area. Now fifteen years old—seven years after the separation—Holden is maturing more successfully. It might alarm you that it took seven years for Holden to recover, but this was a particularly nasty case. If you take care to reduce conflict between you and your spouse, even if your child's behavior becomes problematic during the latter years of your marriage or early in your separation, your child will likely have a much shorter transition and recovery period. Had Holden's parents stayed together and continued to treat each other as poorly as they did when they were married, we think Holden would be in much worse shape today. These days his school performance is beginning to reflect more of his potential. Divorce broke the destructive cycle of conflict and humiliation and allowed some healing in the boy's war-ravaged psyche. Holden's behavior had grown worse during the openly escalating conflict of the two-year postseparation transition period. As the level of conflict declined, so did Holden's problem behaviors.

It is not reasonable to think that all of this boy's problems have been solved. In all likelihood, Holden will bear the scars of his parents' years of conflict for a long time. People may say, "It's because he comes from a divorced family," but this would not be an accurate conclusion. Yes, his family divorced, but his problems with overaggressiveness toward other children, defiance of adults, and poor school performance—all reflective of poor self-esteem—existed long before the breakup. The unhappy, intact family is destructive to children. Teachers of nursery- and elementary-school children whom we interviewed frequently confirmed this. In the words of one: "We know which kids come from troubled families. We see it every day in their attitudes and behavior. We are usually in no position to say anything about it, but we know these marriages are in trouble years before the parents do anything about it, if they ever do."

So what can you take away from Holden's story if you're contemplating divorce? If one or more of your children are having problems, it is likely that open or hidden conflict in your marriage is taking its toll on them. The easiest choice is to do nothing. You may want to assume that your child is going through a difficult stage and that if you sweep it under the rug and ignore it, it will go away. It's a more difficult choice to try to do something about it. If you and your spouse can act in a concerted way to fix things, and jointly work to help your child, then maybe you should stay. That was not an option for Holden's parents.

Getting Worse Before Getting Better

Peter, Sara's father, whom we spoke about earlier, also told us that, at first, after his separation, things got worse for him and Sara. There were plenty of times he felt despair about his daughter's future and the future of his relationship with her:

> After my separation, Sara argued more with me, not less. She continued to get into arguments with her friends and with her teachers in school. She picked the troubled kids for friends. Things between her mother and me also got worse. We were fighting more than ever, although now it was about money and visitation.
>
> When Sara and I would spend time together, she would be sullen and act as if she were doing me a favor. Any activity I suggested she vetoed. If I asked her what she wanted to do, she said, "Nothing." If I told her she was being a pain in the neck, she replied, "Then take me home." As far as I was concerned, I had made a home for her. She had her own room with her own furniture and toys. My apartment was in the town where her friends and school were, and they were welcome to be with her at any time.

Peter went on to say that although things were bad between him and Sara, they soon grew even worse:

> Sara and I had a spat over a minor incident. She called her mother to come and pick her up, which her mother wrongly did, instead of telling Sara to work out the problem with me. My ex-wife arrived with a car full of my former neighbors; would you believe, they taunted me while driving off with Sara? This was the bottom, but I guess it was also a turning point.
>
> I didn't know what to do. I went to a family counselor who had tried to help us once before, and I got great advice from her. She sympathized with me, but she told me not to chase after my daughter. She said she knew it would be painful for me, but she felt that right then Sara didn't want much of a relationship with me because she was caught in the middle between her mother, whom she lived with, and me. The counselor told me not to force myself on Sara, not to bad-mouth her mother, but to keep the door open and my daughter would eventually come around. The counselor

recommended that I see Sara only when my daughter wanted it, and not to force her to see me just to meet the visitation schedule. In hindsight, this turned out to be a cooling-off period for everybody. For about a year I saw a lot less of Sara than I wanted to and was even legally entitled to, but very gradually Sara did come around so that more often we were able to enjoy one another when we were together.

That was four years ago. Sara is now fourteen. She has made several new friends; they're nice kids. She's doing better than ever in school, and my relationship with her is the best it has ever been, even compared with the years before I separated. We enjoy each other more than ever.

The greatest protection you can provide your children's developing self-esteem is to minimize conflict between you and your spouse. That includes both open and covert conflict. If you need professional help to come to agreement with your mate, get it. Have one or two meetings with a counselor to evaluate your problems and how to begin to solve them. If you divorce, keeping conflict between you and your ex to a minimum, as Holden's story illustrates, is critical for your children's mental and emotional health. Remember, it's the conflict that occurs between you and your mate during the marriage, and, if it continues, during the divorce, that injures your child's self-esteem, not the divorce itself.

Questions to Think About

1. Do we often argue about our children? Yes___No___
2. Are we often incapable of pulling together to act jointly to help our child address behavior and school performance issues? Yes___No___

CHAPTER 12

Impact on Adolescents and Young Adults

So far we have been focusing mostly on the effects that divorcing or continuing to live in the unhappy family have on younger children. If you are deciding if it's time to go, you probably have equally serious worries about your adolescent and young adult children. In addition to school and behavioral concerns, you probably are worried about sexual behavior, impaired social life, and drug abuse in your teenagers.

Teens and Sex

One fear of parents who are thinking about separation is that their adolescent girls will become promiscuous. Promiscuity is a problem for several reasons: the social stigma it may create, especially for teenage girls; the damage it may do to the ability to form deep and lasting relationships in adult years; and, of course, the danger promiscuity poses in terms of contracting sexually transmitted diseases and becoming pregnant. Rumors circulate that promiscuity is a common problem among adolescent girls from divorced families. Most research finds this fear to be baseless. Adolescents and young adults from divorced families become sexually active at the same age as children from intact families, and are not likely to have sex with any greater frequency or with more varied partners than their counterparts from intact families.

There is even evidence to demonstrate that it's more common for girls from unhappy, intact families to be promiscuous; they have sex earlier and with more partners than girls from divorced families. Lisa Gabardi and Lee Rosen, as reported in the *Journal of Divorce and Remarriage,* studied college students from divorced and intact families. They interviewed three hundred single, heterosexual eighteen to twenty-five-year-old students at the University of California–Santa Cruz in 1992. They found that being from a divorced or an intact family was not a key variable correlated with the frequency of the students' sexual encounters, their number of sexual partners, or negative attitudes young people had toward marriage. The key variable was their parents' past and ongoing conflict, either in intact or divorced families.

Sexual and social problems are not particularly aggravated by parents divorcing, but are often made worse by kids remaining in the unhappy family, or by continued exposure to conflict between parents following separation.

Research by Rebecca Anne Jones, done at Georgia State University in 1993, also concludes that adolescents from divorced families date as much as those from nondivorced families and that they report enjoying the same levels of satisfaction in dating. Dr. Jones examined the impact of their parents' divorces on 178 college-aged daughters with regard to the age when they first had a boyfriend, how many very short-lived heterosexual relationships they had, and what their level of satisfaction was with their dating relationships. There were no differences on these measures between girls in the study who were from intact families and girls from divorced families, though the girls in the study from divorced families did report that they were less trusting in their relationships with a boyfriend.

We think there are two factors that prompt more sexual activity in adolescents from unhappy families. In some unhappy families, a father who is alienated from his wife may derive warmth and admiration from his adolescent daughter, giving and getting approval that should normally be supplied by his spouse. In these families, the daughter may come to depend on this excessive attention from a older man, especially if the mother has a troubled relationship with her daughter, as often happens when the two females feel as if they're competing for the attention of the husband/father. In cases like these, some young girls from unhappy families enter middle adolescence and begin to date as a way to seek approval outside the family. If such a girl has had a very intense relationship with her father and seeks this same level of intensity too desperately and too quickly with boys who are her peers, this can lead to excessive, inappropriate, or premature sexual encounters.

Daughters in unhappy families may also be vulnerable to becoming promiscuous for another reason. In certain cases, a father is rejecting of both a mother and a daughter, and the daughter is also in conflict with her mother.

Whether you stay or go, your positive relationship with your child is her greatest protection, especially if you are the same-sex parent.

If the daughter then feels that her mom is someone she can't admire, the girl is likely to be starved for affection and love, since the girl doesn't connect well with either parent. She may become sexually active because of her need for a loving, close relationship. This conflict is not likely to be present when a girl enjoys a strong relationship with her mother, who is then able to guide and protect her. Thus a key factor, although not the only factor, for reducing the likelihood of promiscuity among adolescent girls, is the quality of the relationship with Mom. Whether Dad and Mom live together or separately is not a factor in determining girls' sexual behavior. So in deciding if it's time to go, you need to look at your adolescent children and ask yourself if the strains in your marriage are showing up in their sexual and/or social behavior.

We speak about the fears that parents who are considering separating have about promiscuity in their daughters, and not their sons, only because parents, incorrectly, seem more concerned about this in girls than in boys. Boys often develop the same patterns of promiscuity, and for similar reasons. Even though it is commonly overlooked in boys, and even somewhat encouraged, promiscuity has the same negative effects on their ability to form intimate relationships later in life, and, of course, it also exposes them to the danger of sexually transmitted diseases and premature, unplanned, unwanted fathering of a child. So the key variable when it comes to diminishing the likelihood of teenage promiscuity and its associated problems—including teenage pregnancy, sexually transmitted diseases, and emotional strain—is not whether the parents are unhappily together or separated, but a strong, loving, appropriate parent-child relationship, especially with the parent of the same sex.

Teens and Drugs

Along these same lines, a study done in 1999 by the National Center for Addiction and Substance Abuse at Columbia University concluded that drug abuse among American teenagers is significantly more prevalent among those teens who have high conflict with their fathers. The study was released by Joseph A. Califano, Jr., the center's president at that time. Califano was the secretary of Health, Education and Welfare during the Carter administration.

The study results were based on a survey of 2,000 teenagers and 1,000 parents, including 555 interviews with parents and teenagers living in the same households. The survey reported finding that youngsters in divorced families headed by a single parent, where the kids have a good relationship with the parent they live with, and little conflict with the noncustodial parent, have the same likelihood of drug abuse as the normal teen population from intact families. But kids who live in intact families where there is a poor relationship between them and their father are at 68 percent greater risk of abusing alcohol and drugs than teenagers from single-parent families where there is a good relationship with the custodial parent. Dr. Alan Leshner, director of the National Institute on Drug Abuse at the time of the survey, commented that the lesson from the study is that "Bad parenting is worse than no parenting." In other words, bad parenting in a two-parent intact household is worse than good parenting in a single-parent household.

The key factor, although not the only factor, in whether teens abuse drugs is the frequency and severity of conflict with Dad—not whether Dad and Mom live together or separately.

Impact on Young Adults

In addition to all the worries you have over your adolescents, you may also have concerns about your young adult children in the age range of twenty-one to thirty. If you are considering whether it is time to go, you want to know if your divorce would make your children more likely to go through divorces of their own. According to the U.S. Census Bureau, young adults from divorced families marry at the same age and at the same rate as their peers from intact homes. They do not divorce any more frequently than those who grew up in intact families. In other words, if you divorce, your children are no more likely to get a divorce than anyone else. Once again, young adult children who develop the most strongly negative attitudes toward marriage come from families where there is or was a high level of conflict. Conflict is key, not whether the parents' marriage is still intact or they are divorced, according to Lisa Gabardi and Lee Rosen. You'll recall that this finding was based on their interviews with three hundred college students aged eighteen to twenty-five, and is yet another indication of the damage caused by the unhappy family.

When we interview adults who grew up in unhappy, intact families and who never want to marry, they say that they don't want to repeat what they went through growing up. Many people choose to stay in unhappy marriages until their children are grown. Our advice is that after five years of efforts to rescue your failing marriage, including getting professional help for at least a year, you need to think about the lifelong consequences of *not* divorcing, for both you and your children.

Fear of Abandonment and Trust

Grown children of divorce do show, to a greater extent than their peers from unhappy families, a tendency to worry more that they will make a bad choice and their love relationships will break up. Judith Wallerstein writes about this in *The Unexpected Legacy of Divorce*. This worry is often persistent and troubling, adding a measure of insecurity to these romantic relationships. This is not altogether bad, insofar as it provides them with strong motivation not to take their relationships for granted. Both for people who grew up in unhappy homes, and for children of divorce, developing a trusting relationship with a partner is one of the most challenging problems of their lives. That said, there is research by Kent Kawagoe at the University of Kansas in a 1992 dissertation to support the conclusion that young adults from divorced families actually have *less difficulty* in developing trust in relationships than do their peers who grew up in unhappy intact families. Kawagoe studied over two hundred college students, half from divorced families and half from intact families. He reported that removing children from the day-to-day alienation and mistrust in an unhappy marriage actually protects their ability to form trusting relationships.

We heard this from Meryl, who had grown up decades before in a chronically unhappy family. "I grew up in a family of enemies," Meryl, a divorced and now-remarried businesswoman, told us. She went on to summarize her family history:

> My parents are very competitive with one another. Each one is constantly trying to prove himself right and the other one wrong. My father has no respect for my mother as a woman, or his wife, and vice versa. What they seem to respect is power, retaliation, or the withholding of love and approval. My parents fight about money endlessly; they are constantly second-guessing one another about spending a dime. I probably have done a

> lot of the same thing. I find it very difficult to be in a partnership, especially when it comes to money. For me not having to answer to anyone else about money is freedom.
>
> My parents have been married forever. After growing up with their continuous battles, their mutual disrespect, and their constant undermining of each other, I think it has been very difficult for me to let my guard down enough to make a good marriage. How was I supposed to learn to trust in the middle of what my father calls "World War III"? Should my parents have divorced? I can't imagine it could have been worse for any of us, and it might have been better. Neither of them has had love, and my sister and I have been struggling to find it also.

The famous psychoanalyst Carl Jung said that "Love and power are shadows of each other. Where love exists power does not, and where power exists love cannot." Meryl finds it very difficult to trust another person enough to give up power. She finds it almost impossible to love.

Questions to Think About

1. Are my spouse and I engaged in a power struggle? Yes___No___
2. Do I worry about the quality of my relationship with my son or daughter? Yes___No___
3. Do I worry about the quality of my spouse's relationship with our son or daughter? Yes___No___

CHAPTER 13

Growth of Empathy in Adolescents and Young Adults

The ancient Greeks said that out of suffering comes wisdom. We believe that the suffering that children of divorce experience can also produce meaningful growth. Children of divorce are asked to develop the sensitivity and flexibility to fit into two different households with two different sets of rules, even two different sets of values. Most of them succeed very well. The stepfamilies we have met include stepbrothers and -sisters, sometimes dramatically younger or older, or sometimes exactly the same age. Forging relationships with these "strangers" and their cousins, aunts, uncles, and grandparents would be a challenge for any of us.

The demand for great sensitivity is also evident in that children of divorce tend to worry about and feel responsible for their parents more than children from intact families. They worry about a parent who is alone being lonely; they worry about their parents' social lives, even passing judgment on whom they are dating. They may worry about their parents' financial well-being. We are not saying that it is good or fair for very young people to have these burdens—it is not—but then divorce is a trade-off. Much good can result, but at a price.

Greater Flexibility

Most children see things in black and white. Yours probably do, too. There is pressure on children from divorced families to learn to see shades of gray. Divorce helps children to develop greater flexibility in their roles and their view of the roles of others in the family. For children of divorce, rigid divisions between traditionally male and female roles tend to blur. This stands to reason because these children witness each of their parents assuming new and often unfamiliar roles and responsibilities, many of which were formerly those of the other partner. Dad is now doing the laundry and cooking, and Mom is balancing her checkbook or doing her tax return for the first time. The children also assume new roles and responsibilities themselves; the only child in one family can become the eldest of five in a new stepfamily.

Meeting the challenges that divorce poses often stimulates children to greater maturity and empathy than their peers from intact families.

Increased Emotional Maturity

Divorce researcher Paul Amato has spent much of his career studying the effects of parental divorce on children's emotional maturity. In an article in the journal *Social Forces,* Amato describes the increase in emotional maturity in the thousands of children he studied that occurred a few years after their parents' divorce. John Gottman, also a highly respected researcher, found the same result and reported it in an article in the well-respected journal *Developmental Psychology.*

We witnessed this maturity when we interviewed Raoul, a twenty-eight-year-old graduate student. He told us that he admired his father and had wanted to live with him when his parents split up around the time Raoul was twelve. Raoul said his father was an exciting person to be with—an artist and a rock radio announcer with an unconventional lifestyle. In Raoul's view, this was a stark contrast to his mother, who was a bookkeeper and a homemaker. Raoul, like his father, rejected her conventionality. Although he wanted to, Raoul couldn't live with his father because his father was moving in with another woman who did not want the responsibility of a young boy. So Raoul reluctantly accepted living in what he considered a much less exciting situation.

Raoul told us a story that was memorable and important to him. It occurred when he was about fourteen, two years after his parents broke up:

> I remember my mother decided that she wanted to buy her first new car. So we went to a Honda showroom and the salesman, Henry, showed us these different cars.
>
> She brought me along for moral support because she was terrified of doing this alone. We went through all the paperwork with the salesman, who kept asking more questions: "Do you want a two-door or a four-door? Four or six cylinders? CD player or not?" The decisions were just wearing her down.

It was absolutely brutal. Then at the last moment she had to decide what color her car was going to be. She broke down in tears, crying and crying and crying. Henry left the office, and she and I had a long talk about what it would be like to have cars of different colors in our driveway. We went through all the options, and finally decided on blue. You know my mother paints for a hobby. It's absurd that somebody with her sense of color would have trouble making this decision, but it was the final decision about buying this car, which was somehow still just a little bit too big a decision at that moment.

I think that for me buying the car was the first big decision I had ever been involved in, more as a friend than as her son. It was the first time I understood how enormously much she had relied on my father's quick judgment and his ability to make decisions. My father would have said: "Let's get a blue car." And that would have been that.

The last time I went back to Arizona, she picked me up in a brand-new car that she had bought the week before. She didn't even tell me about this new car she had gotten when I had spoken to her on the phone. It was fine. She decided she wanted a car. She bought a car.

Raoul's response to his parents' divorce was to grow up faster. In this incident he was able to be his mother's "friend," patiently helping her to visualize what each car color would look like. It is also striking that Raoul in no way judged his mother. He did not judge her tentativeness at making each choice, her emotionalism, or her struggle with being a woman making what might have been considered in the past a man's decision. He didn't even judge his mother for not acting like a mother at that moment. She didn't have ready answers. She needed his support. These qualities of maturity, empathy, and flexibility in the role he played in this situation are rare in fourteen-year-olds.

Divorce challenges children to rise to the occasion. Studies by David Gately working under Professor Andrew Schwebel in the Department of Psychology at Ohio State University in 1993 found that most children succeed, much of the time. They reported on their "challenge model for favorable outcomes" in the *Journal of Divorce and Remarriage*. In interviews with both elementary- and secondary- school–aged children, and their divorced parents, the two researchers found that by their own and their parents' observations the children persistently rose to the challenges they were presented as a result of their parents' divorces. They found that children who experienced divorce are surprisingly resilient and show increased strengths that often include greater maturity, greater self-esteem, empathy, and flexibility, compared with their preseparation levels of development.

Bruce, whose situation we described earlier, sees this same process occurring with his son Holden. Holden's mom's cat has grown old. The cat recently suffered a seizure that left her unable to control her bladder. The veterinarian cannot do anything to restore the cat's health and Holden's mom's apartment has begun to smell bad. Still, she can't seem to make the decision to put the cat to sleep. Holden feels that it would be better for everyone to take this step, even though he also loves the cat. Bruce said he was amazed at the level of understanding and compassion Holden showed, talking about his mother's tremendous reluctance to come to this conclusion. Holden told Bruce that with patience Holden believes he will help her to make the decision. In a few years it seems that Holden has come a long way.

Questions to Think About

1. Am I afraid that our children will be burdened with worry if I divorce? Yes___No___

2. Do I stay, in part, because I don't feel I am capable of making all the decisions that I would have to make solo if I divorced? Yes___No___

How Men and Women Grow

Think of your friends who have divorced. Have you noticed that, after separating, the woman whose husband lamented about how boring and dull she had become over the years suddenly has gone back to school or become involved in a sport or volunteer work? Have you noticed that the guy whose wife used to complain bitterly that he spent all his free time glued to the TV watching sports is suddenly taking a new girlfriend to movies, restaurants, and the stadium? Think about what your spouse has been actively asking you to do, or might be too afraid of hurting your feelings to ask you to do.

In an unhappy marriage, it is common for each of you to berate or nag one another about perceived shortcomings. Maybe one of you accuses the other of being cheap or sloppy; insensitive; too cautious; or tied to your e-mail, cell phone, or the office. Because of the power struggles that are common in an unhappy marriage, when one spouse is criticized, he usually defends himself against the perceived attack, and angrily rejects the criticism. The unhappiness of the marriage undermines motivation for change and makes people resistant and stubborn. It doesn't have to be that way. Wouldn't you be better off making the changes now that might save your marriage, rather than making them after the marriage is over?

What keeps you from wanting to make the changes your mate wants from you? Many people we interviewed lack the motivation to change because doing so is never easy and they don't believe their spouse would ever leave them. They don't take these nagging issues as seriously as they should. Many people take their marriage for granted. The poet e.e. cummings wrote, "Be of love more careful than of anything." We think he was trying to warn us not to be surprised that we have driven love away by assuming it will always be there, no matter how careless or stubborn we are.

Delayed Compliance

We have identified a phenomenon we call *delayed compliance*. It is a powerful motivator toward growth and change that occurs in many separated and divorced people. Stan and Frances are a perfect example.

When Frances left Stan, her husband of twenty years, he was in a state of shock. He had thought that things were "good enough" between them, so that the thought of Frances leaving him was next to impossible. Then on her BlackBerry he discovered sexually explicit e-mails that Frances had been exchanging with another man. He confronted her and she admitted that she had been having an affair for some time, and that she wanted out of the marriage. By her account, she and Stan, who had no children, had been leading completely separate lives for more than a decade.

Earlier in their marriage, she had been critical of Stan's obsession with food, both cooking and eating, and the weight he gained over the early years. She had worried about his health, and had been upset that he didn't care about his appearance. Because he had repeatedly ignored her, she had lapsed into alienated silence. Stan also had given up his criticisms of Frances's self-absorption, her lack of interest in his business, and what he called her fanaticism about physical fitness and a youthful appearance. Stan had drowned his alienation from Frances in more cooking and more eating and in his work in his furniture-manufacturing business. In the last ten years he had gained well over a hundred pounds onto an already stocky frame. Frances, who works in the fashion business, had become so distant from her husband that she thought she had stopped caring.

Stan fell apart when Frances left him. He couldn't go to work; most days he didn't even get out of bed. He even talked about whether life was worth living anymore. Frances, who at first had planned to continue seeing her lover, felt terribly guilty. She didn't hate Stan, and she was petrified that he might lose his business, or worse.

After several tearful telephone conversations, he convinced her to come over to the house, and they stayed up an entire night, the first of several, talking honestly to each other. Frances told Stan how physically unattractive he had become to her over the years because of his weight gain and her worries about his health. Writing in *Family Therapy Networker,* marriage counselor David Schnarch aptly calls these extremely honest conversations the "crucible." A crucible is a container used in gold smelting. It is heated to very high temperatures in order to burn off the impurities, leaving pure gold.

Stan talked to Frances about her lack of interest in him, and her lack of interest in anything except her business and her appearance. They both confessed how stubborn each of them felt, and how each one had been waiting for years for the other to make moves of reconciliation. Each had been refusing to budge and was leaving it to the other to make an effort on behalf of the marriage. Neither had made an effort, until Stan accidentally discovered the e-mails, which precipitated the crisis. Frances agreed to return on a trial basis if they would go into couples counseling and explore what had gone wrong between them. Stan also decided to go on a diet.

After two years, they are still in counseling. Frances agreed to stop all contact with the other man. Stan has lost over one hundred pounds, and Frances is very proud of him. She finds him attractive again. They have become better partners to each other. Frances has been much more willing to take time off and to relax, and they have enjoyed several vacations together, something they hadn't done in the previous decade. They are not entirely out of the woods, but they are making progress, trying to better meet each other's needs in the marriage.

Had Frances and Stan divorced, they may have made some of the changes they have made anyway. Frances's relationship with another man would not have thrived any better if she had remained so self-involved, and Stan might have decided to lose weight to be better able to go forward in a new life. Rather than delaying compliance, they made their choice to make the changes their marriage needed in order to restart it. It took a shock—one that happened accidentally—to get Stan and Frances to begin reversing the breakdown in their marriage. To say they caught it in the nick of time would be an understatement. Most people whose marriages are so far gone aren't as fortunate.

No More Need to Defend

People usually don't change until it's too late to save their marriage. This is the *delay* in *delayed compliance*. It is when people eventually make changes that they recognize are in their best interest after the marriage is over.

If you are motivated to change—whether it's in time to save your marriage or even after your marriage is over—you are nonetheless one of the lucky ones. Sadly, divorce doesn't come with a guarantee of a future, happier life. Unless you are able to do the difficult work of taking some responsibility for your share of the problems that are leading to the failure of your relationship, you are in some danger of repeating them, even though you swear to yourself you will pick someone different next time. As we said earlier, people divorce in second marriages at approximately the same rate as in first marriages. This is why it is so important to look at yourself and what you are contributing to the breakdown, even if you feel as if you're the one who has been the victim.

Why do people change after it's too late to save their marriage? Perhaps it's because they see themselves more clearly after a separation, or because they no longer need to defend themselves so fiercely, or because no one is criticizing them anymore.

We all run the risk of casting ourselves as victims of our spouses, rather than taking responsibility for our part in creating the problems in our marriages.

Even if your partner has been unfaithful, which is obviously terribly painful, if you look at yourself honestly you may be able to see some of the ways in which you disappointed your partner or let him down. This doesn't justify his behavior. Still, his behavior probably came about, in part, because he didn't tell you what was troubling him or, if he did, you couldn't hear it. While it may be difficult, try to hear your spouse's complaints about you, especially when he voices the same or similar ones repeatedly. Maybe you couldn't listen until now, but it might not be too late. Doing this with the help of a professional counselor can make the process a lot more effective.

Jerry told us he left Tika for many reasons, among them that he couldn't stand what he experienced as her paranoid, guarded, and overly cautious approach to life. She seemed to be afraid of anything new, anything out of her daily routine. Traveling was an especially sore point between them. Jerry had always believed that he would see the world if he could earn a good enough living to do so. Although they could afford to take trips, and could organize work and child supervision to allow for travel, Tika vetoed almost any plan that Jerry proposed.

Jerry laughed as he told us that in the five years since their divorce, "Tika has certainly changed. She has traveled to England, France, Spain,

Morocco, and New York, several times to Florida and to Vermont, all from her home in California." This is an example of delayed compliance.

Lauren told us she had a similar experience after divorcing Jim. She complained for years to Jim about his passivity. When his mom died and left him some money, he retired in his early forties, while Lauren was still working full time. Even though they had enough money, Jim kept paring down their expenses so they could live on less and less. It wasn't the money that troubled Lauren; it was the "nothingness of Jim's life," as Lauren put it. Jim had stopped playing poker with his friends, whom he had played with for years. He had stopped working out, or being interested in volunteering his time, which he had done on some occasions previously, or "initiating anything." Lauren bought him a gym membership; she signed them up for dance lessons, and made one recommendation after another to try to enliven him and their life together. Nothing budged Jim. After years of trying to "breathe life" into Jim, she left. They had been married for fifteen years.

In the year after they split up, Jim was out night after night. He took golf lessons. He reconnected with his long-lost male friends. He volunteered to teach reading to illiterate adults, and lots of other things. Jim is a prime example of delayed compliance. If he had done half of this during the marriage, Lauren said, they probably would still be together.

Think it over. Should you decide it's time to go, what are you likely to want to change about yourself and your approach to life? Would you lose weight? Would you try an antidepressant to get yourself out of your funk? Would you get additional child care so you could enjoy a more active social life? Would you organize your household, increase your income, stop spending so much time with your parents in favor of making new friends, stop devoting yourself exclusively to your career, or take a bigger interest in and spend more time with your children? Are these things your spouse wishes you would do now? Why wait? Perhaps making changes now will break a logjam between you and your spouse before divorce, rather than after it.

How Divorced Women Grow

Women initiate more than two out of three separations and divorces. Do they leave because they have been abused? For the most part, no. While numbers vary with sources from a low of 6 percent to a high of 20 percent, abuse is not the main reason women leave their marriages. Do they leave because of their husband's infidelity? No. Husbands are cited in divorce only slightly more often than wives are for infidelity.

Growing Apart

Law professor Margaret Brinig from George Mason University and economist Douglas Allen from Simon Fraser University in Vancouver, Canada, reported in the *American Law and Economics Review* their study of all 46,000 divorces during the year 1995 filed in four states (Connecticut, Virginia, Montana, Oregon—the only four states in the United States that collect this information). They found that divorce is most frequently initiated by the better-educated partner. They also found that two out of three divorces were initiated by women. According to Brinig and Allen, people initiating the divorce often reported that they felt they had outgrown their mate, and that their partner had made little or no effort to advance themselves or grow during the marriage. The bottom line is that the cause of conflict in a marriage, and one of the most common reasons people divorce, is that they have long felt stifled in the relationship, and that if they stay, their lives will be an empty shell and a sham. These people often say they have no choice but to leave if they want to thrive. Women in these states felt this way twice as frequently as men.

In 25 percent of the breakups, the men reported that they had no clue that there was a problem in their marriage. Many fewer women reported this. Brinig and Allen reported that women said they entered marriage for very different reasons than men. Women frequently stated that they believed that marriage would be an extension of courtship, continuing the romance and the relationship. Men, on the other hand, in Brinig and Allen's survey, expected that marriage would provide "sex, home, food, and children." Romance and relationship were not high on men's lists as reasons for marrying. This gives an understanding of why so many men reported little idea that there were problems in their marriages. These men were getting what they expected: sex, home, food, and children. Their wives were apparently not getting what they expected: romance and relationship.

Unanticipated Findings

While outgrowing one's partner was the most frequent reason for divorcing, Brinig and Allen, perhaps surprisingly, found that abuse was cited in only

6 percent of all divorce filings in the four states that were studied. The study further reports that adultery was named as the cause of the breakup 20 percent of the time, and accusations of adultery were approximately evenly split between men and women seeking divorces.

The researchers report that both men and women see children as the greatest asset of their marriage. They demonstrated that in the states where sole custody of the children was routinely awarded to the woman, women filed for divorce much more commonly than they did in states where joint custody was more prevalent. Brinig and Allen point out that women's greater likelihood of initiating divorce, in part, reflects their anticipation of getting sole custody. They also found that in communities where divorce is more common, women are not afraid of the stigma traditionally associated with a marital breakup, and file for divorce more often. Where divorce is less common, a lower percentage of women file for divorce.

Improved Well-Being

An important consideration in how to know if it's time to go is knowing what is likely to happen to you if you're a woman and you choose to divorce. Women—even more than men or children—report that their lives are better after they have divorced. In their book *Divorce,* Allison Clarke-Stewart and Dr. Cornelia Brentano reported that 72 percent of the divorced women they interviewed told them they experienced improved emotional well-being, and an increased sense of independence and self-confidence within three years after their divorce. You'll recall that Wallerstein and Hetherington each separately found very similar levels of satisfaction among separated and divorced women.

Three out of four women feel that divorce has improved their lives within a couple of years of separating. This is particularly true among women who have strong support networks of family, friends, and at work.

Rebuilding Self-Esteem

Most people underestimate their abilities and their capacities because of a lack of confidence in themselves. Add to this the daily debilitating disregard and disrespect of an unhappy marriage and self-confidence will plummet. On the first day after separation, the need to assume new responsibilities and call on newfound inner strengths begins.

Research by psychologist Nancy Fischer at the University of

Pennsylvania and Dr. Doris Stormoen at the University of Wisconsin shows just this. Both found that after a transition period, most divorcing women feel better about themselves, are more independent, feel more competent, and have improved relationships with their family and friends. This is especially true of women who keep full or shared custody of their children, despite the stresses of being a single parent.

The discovery that you possess the ability to cope with a multitude of demands, many of which are brand new, or, at the very least, greatly expanded from your previous experience, creates a powerful sense of competence and independence.

A study by Teresa Sakraida, working at the Catholic University of America, studied 154 women from Indiana and Pennsylvania who had been divorced less than two years, and who had been married more than three years. All the women were between the ages of thirty-four and fifty-four. Sakraida's interviews show that the person who seeks the divorce tends to exhibit more growth and more development of new capacities after separation, including, most commonly, returning to school, learning new personal skills, and taking on new or expanded employment. So, if you decide it's time to go, even though the road is likely to be difficult, these are some of the benefits you are likely to experience if you allow yourself to rise to the occasion and are willing to take on new challenges. Most divorcing women do.

Independence and Love

Frieda worried about just what it was her husband was doing to earn so much money. She could never really get a straight answer out of him to the basic question of "What exactly do you do for a living?" But Frieda learned not to ask too many questions so she could enjoy their affluent lifestyle, which included his Mercedes sports car and spur-of-the-moment trips to the Bahamas or Las Vegas. But what troubled Frieda greatly through it all was not where the money was coming from, but that she suspected that her husband was unfaithful. Sometimes he didn't come home at night. Sometimes he came home intoxicated. He always had excuses; he was a fast talker. She was intimidated by him, dependent on him financially, and critical of herself for feeling this way.

When she found a condom in his pants pocket, she couldn't deny her suspicions anymore. She confronted him, but he had no satisfactory responses, nor any remorse, just more fast talk. She started planning how she would leave him, although she was frightened that he might try to hurt her. She eventually mustered the courage to leave, and started divorce proceedings. In the settlement she got enough money from him to buy a small condominium apartment and enough money to live on carefully for a couple of years. Frieda was smart. She returned to school and got a degree in accounting. After she graduated, she landed a job in a large accounting firm. Within a few years she met another accountant, and they fell in love and got married. Frieda lives at a comfortable financial level. Though it is well below the luxurious lifestyle she experienced with her first husband, she is proud of her accomplishments, loves her work, and loves her husband. She tells us that she has never been happier.

Maturation and Development

In some respects, like Frieda's husband, Parker refused to treat his wife as an adult. When Florence and Parker's marriage was coming apart, he would throw up his hands during arguments and cry out, "What happened to the little girl I married?" Although Florence was a nursery school teaching assistant and a parent, she did not participate in any financial or other important decisions in the marriage, and was accountable to Parker for her time, her expenses, any friendships she maintained, how they were raising their son, and how she kept house.

Parker resisted any changes Florence wanted to make that would allow her to mature. She wanted to go back to school to finish her degree and qualify for her teaching license. She no longer felt content to account for every moment she spent with women friends. She felt increasingly imprisoned by Parker's ultratraditional views of what marriage should be like. She no longer was willing to be characterized as a "little girl"; she was a thirty-two-year-old woman. They persistently argued about these things until Florence ultimately left, taking their little son and not much else. When women are asked why they initiate divorce, they often don't articulate it specifically, but many describe tensions surrounding rigid gender-based roles in their marriages. Researchers often find that couples refer to these types of problems as "differences in values."

Florence's finances were strained during the transitional years after her divorce. Out of anger and resentment for her "betrayal" of him, Parker vigorously fought against providing generous support for her and their child. Forced to manage her finances independently, Florence discovered that she had an entrepreneurial streak. Not only did she get her teaching certification, but she eventually opened her own small preschool and managed to make a go of it.

Growth for Divorced Men

Sakraida's 2002 study collected data on men as well. She reported that many men are unprepared for divorce, whereas women usually contemplate it for quite some time. Many men don't tend to have the close relationships with family and friends or the household skills that would make the transition easier for them.

Parker was shocked and crushed when Florence left. He went into counseling and moved near Florence and their little boy. He became quite devoted to the child, perhaps for the first time. Florence points out that after he got over his feelings of rejection he seemed to grow into a more flexible person. Five years later, Parker married again and had another child. He and his second wife seem to have a more equal relationship than he had with Florence. He is a devoted father to each of his children.

Children Help

Allison Clarke-Stewart and Cornelia Brentano's research finds that the transition period takes about two or three years for men. After that, at least two out of three men who have divorced experience gains in self-esteem and also speak of greater satisfaction with their lives. The greatest gains are among fathers who remain actively involved with their children. More than 75 percent of divorced fathers with children under eighteen pay child support (even Parker did, although grudgingly).

It makes sense that creating a home for yourself and your child after a marital breakup provides your life with organization and meaning. Parenting forces a man to form routines, eat regular meals, and maintain a semblance of home life. Even if the father is not the custodial parent, these activities contribute to his personal stability, growth, and self-esteem.

According to professors of sociology at Brandeis University, Harry Keshet and Kristine Rosenthal, meeting the demands of child care and child support contributes greatly to a divorced man's stability and personal growth.

Earnings Increase

During the first seven years after a divorce, men of all incomes, but especially those with low incomes, increase their earnings substantially if they pay child support consistently. This was found in a 1991 study conducted at the University of Wisconsin by Dr. Elizabeth Phillips and Dr. Irwin Garfinkel. Apparently, men who consistently pay child support are spurred by a sense of responsibility and a desire to maintain their lifestyle, so they work harder and longer.

Sex Role Stereotypes Break Down

Many men are also forced to abandon rigid sex role stereotypes once they divorce. This contributes to their flexibility and adaptation. It forces them to mature and gives them feelings of greater competence. A recent award-winning South African film, *Tsotse,* tells the tragic tale of a young hoodlum and murderer named Tsotse who hijacks an automobile, only to find out that the screaming woman whom he forced from the car had her sleeping infant son in a car seat in the back of the car. Several minutes later, when he has driven the car far from the scene of the crime and the mother, Tsotse discovers his predicament. He is now a kidnapper, but he has also unwittingly become the foster parent of an infant boy. The film is about the development of Tsotse's sense of humanity and responsibility. Tsotse finds the protective, tender, and caring side of himself. He has little hope of returning the child to his parents without risking prison. Eventually, he does return the child.

Men tend to remarry fairly quickly after divorce. They report that they select second wives who are more fun and more flexible, whom they have more in common with, and with whom they enjoy better sex.

In his research, Richard Straight at the University of Western Michigan identifies this vulnerable and tender "soft" side of men. He observes that men suffer greater stress over the loss of the marital relationship than women, and are therefore more motivated to find a new love relationship.

Andrew told us he balked when his first wife, Jane, wanted to go to graduate school to study educational administration. She was a successful young teacher and she wanted to become a principal, and then, perhaps, teach at the college level. They had no children and she was very ambitious. He wasn't ashamed to tell her that "No wife of mine will ever hold a higher degree than I have." Three years later Jane divorced him. He told us that she felt he was rigid and unreasonable and that the graduate school issue was just one of many important conflicts they had about her desire to achieve in her career and to be independent.

Andrew was devastated. He loved Jane, and he didn't believe in divorce. He felt that he had offered her a lot. He was handsome, young, financially successful, and reasonably well educated himself. After the divorce, he went out with a lot of women. He reports that he spent years hanging on to his rigid, sexist, and patriarchal values. Still, he never fell in love with anyone who shared those values, was willing to fall into line with them, and wanted a traditional relationship. Eventually, he decided to marry again. The woman he chose for his second wife, Karen, is the only woman besides Jane who would stand up to him. He says he has come to understand that, in fact, that's what he respects and is attracted to. Karen is also a career woman, like Jane. Andrew has changed. He is committed to a new approach. When they were engaged, Andrew said to Karen, "If I mess this up and act like a stubborn mule, please don't divorce me. Shoot me." Since they are together, he has coached Karen to advance her career. With Andrew's guidance and support, Karen is so successful that she outearns him and he has no problem with that. This is also an example of delayed compliance. Andrew learned from what he had done wrong with Jane and became determined not to repeat his mistakes.

Questions to Think About

1. Am I aware of changes that my spouse has repeatedly wanted me to make and I have been unable or unwilling to make?
   Yes___No___

2. Am I aware of changes I have repeatedly wanted my spouse to make that he or she has been unable or unwilling to make?
   Yes___No___

3. Could it be that stubbornness, defensiveness, and resistance to criticism are preventing both of us from changing?
   Yes___No___

4. Do I think that my spouse dismisses some of my concerns because she doesn't believe I would ever leave our marriage?
   Yes___No___

5. Have we avoided the "crucible" of completely open and honest conversation about our problems? Yes___No___
6. Do I feel I have outgrown my mate? Yes___No___
7. Do I feel my self-confidence has been hurt by the disregard and/ or disrespect in my marriage? Yes___No___
8. Do I feel my maturation, growth, and development as a person, as a professional, or as a parent have been hindered by my marriage? Yes___No___

CHAPTER 15

Divorce and Finances

Step 8: Face your fears—What financial repercussions of separation and divorce frighten me?

If you are a woman and you are trying to decide if it's time to go, you are undoubtedly wondering what impact divorcing will have on your finances. There are opinions to support almost any argument you may want to make about what happens to women's finances after divorce. More to the point are a number of questions that it is important for you to ask yourself if you are thinking about whether it is time to go:

- *What stage of life are you in?* How old are you? Are you young enough to make a new beginning, perhaps finish or extend your education, or start to build a career? Are you old enough so that you have built a career, or saved some money that could provide you with a safety net? Are you in the middle of your life without many resources, but prepared to make sacrifices in order to be free of a marriage you can no longer sustain?
- *Can you and your spouse reach a reasonable financial arrangement?* Will your spouse fight you for every dollar, or will he want you to be all right financially? Can you tolerate a bitter dispute if your husband or wife forces one? Do you have the stomach for it? Is there really enough money or assets and income to divide between the two of you to maintain something near your current lifestyle? Can you accept living at a standard lower than your current lifestyle for an indeterminate period? How attached are you to your material "stuff"? Can you live relatively happily without some of it, even without much of it?

- *How employable are you?* What skills or experience do you have to fall back on? If you have children, how old are they? What alternatives can you generate for child care if you go to work, or work longer hours than you do currently?
- *Can you look for help elsewhere?* Would or could your parents or other relatives provide a safety net for you if you were in a financial bind? Could you see yourself using this as a resource? Is there another person in your life you could live with and share expenses with—a sibling, a friend, another relative, a lover?

If you do decide to go, it may seem obvious that in the near term you and your spouse will need to support two households with the same income with which you two have supported one, but the realities are more complicated, and not necessarily as bad as you might imagine.

Not Economic Victims

There is ample evidence to contradict the widely held views that many women fall into poverty as a result of divorce. It's important to mention again that the most commonly quoted statistics on women's finances after divorce—that they decline 73 percent—was from the work of Professor Lenore Weitzman at Harvard University. It took Dr. Weitzman eleven years, but she eventually acknowledged that her claims were false and were in error. Dr. Weitzman acknowledged this ten years ago. Yet these numbers continue to be repeated by interest groups who seek to frighten women into believing them. This is obviously an emotionally charged and controversial subject. Dr. Weitzman was in error, but she is not alone. There remain strong feelings among varied groups of people that many women, particularly poor and working-class women, are economic victims of divorce.

A False Excuse

The myth that women are frequently economic victims of divorce has serious repercussions for the women who buy into it. Some women resign themselves to living in desolate or abusive marriages, paralyzed by the fear that they will take too steep a drop in their standard of living if they leave and receive no support from their husbands. A man we interviewed described his parents' story. His father is an affluent real estate broker in a large Canadian city. He has to go out several evenings a week to entertain prospective buyers. His wife has usually accompanied him to these dinners. On these occasions, he often makes fun of her, teases her, and makes jokes at her expense in front of their guests. He apparently thinks he is being playful, his son told us. He'll say things like: "We've been married thirty years, feels like sixty." The wife typically keeps silent; she doesn't fight back. She gets revenge by being cold to her husband and spending large amounts of money on things they don't need.

The son has told us that over the years his parents' marriage has continued to deteriorate. His father's open disrespect for his wife has increased. His mother's feelings of alienation, self-deprecation, and helplessness continue to grow. Lately, the husband has begun inviting young attractive women brokers to the business dinners along with his wife and flaunting his seeming involvement with them to his wife's deep humiliation. We asked the son why his mother stays in this unacceptable situation. He told us, "I have asked my mother that question again and again. She always brushes the question off, and says she is incapable of making a life for herself on her own, and she doesn't want to give up being affluent."

He also says that he has asked his father several times why he doesn't leave. He isn't happily married either, and he complains to his son that his wife is extremely cold. His son thinks it is because he doesn't want to give up a lot of money in a divorce settlement, but he also tells his son that he doesn't believe that anyone else would put up with him. His son tells us that he knows that the financial excuse is phony, and that there is ample money for both of them.

Returning to Your Standard of Living

Contrary to widespread popular belief, U.S. Census Bureau figures reveal that, after a transition period, 75 percent of all women who divorce experience little if any drop in their standard of living, and the majority of the 25 percent of women who do experience a drop, rebound financially within a few years through a combination of personal income growth, including improved employment, alimony, child support, property settlements, and/or remarriage.

If you were living at a level that people would call working class, divorce is not likely to change that. If you were living at or below the poverty line, divorce is not likely to change that. And if you live a solidly middle class

Within a few years of their divorce, approximately nine out of ten women return to roughly the same standard of living that they had during their marriages.

life, divorce isn't likely to change that, either. The same holds true if you are very affluent.

Also keep in mind that research done by Kathleen O'Connell-Corcoran at the Center for Dispute Resolution at Southern Methodist University demonstrated that about 75 percent of women who retain shared or full custody of their children receive child support, and that this number keeps growing annually because the courts have become increasingly strict in enforcing child support and alimony payments. Thus, so-called "deadbeat (divorced) dads" are much rarer than we are led to believe by the popular media.

The term *deadbeat dads* is an unfortunate one. The Southern Methodist University study also found that the majority of the 25 percent of dads who do not pay child support and alimony are from among the working and unemployed poor. Most of these are men with incomes of under $30,000 a year. Half of them have incomes of under $15,000 a year. They need every penny merely to get by. The number of middle- or upper-middle-class "deadbeat dads" is very small. However, men in this small group, who mostly refuse to fulfill their obligations, especially the more affluent among them, get all the media attention for being irresponsible, cruel, and insensitive—and they deserve it.

Potential for Positive Life Changes

The women we interviewed were mostly successful in rebounding financially after divorce. Those who did all persevered, were creative, and eventually adapted well to their new financial situation. Some returned to school, others rediscovered a talent, thus improving their employment prospects. Some women changed everything; for example, moving to a new part of the country or entering a business and lifestyle they had no former connection with at all. Some women benefited by taking themselves more seriously, and making a greater commitment to work than they had in the past. Those who didn't prosper often seemed to us to be resigned, passive, and too accepting of whatever situation they found themselves in.

If you decide it's time to go, the lesson we have learned from many women is that you must persevere in trying to bring your finances and standard of living back to your current level.

Returning to School

Josephine had recently arrived in New York City from Puerto Rico when her husband left her and their daughter. She had no money, but fortunately she was eligible for various government assistance programs. For the first year, she supplemented the assistance by working on and off as a waitress, while her cousin helped her out with babysitting. Josephine didn't think this life had much promise for her or her child. She applied to a program for nursing and was awarded a scholarship. She made her way through the program with the continued help of her cousin, government assistance, and part-time work. Josephine has now established herself in a satisfying career as a nurse. She is a very compassionate human being and has specialized in health care for the homeless and care for patients with AIDS. She has seen to it that her daughter is a diligent student in school, and, while she hasn't remarried, she is in a relationship with a physician whom she met through her work.

Rediscovering a Talent

When Kay's husband left her and her young daughter, she had no job and no money. The only thing she had was a large loft space they had bought in an out-of-the-way neighborhood in Miami. Kay had been totally financially dependent on her husband. He was not her daughter's father, so she could not get any child support from him, and in order to keep her home, the loft, she agreed to forgo any alimony. Kay is a vivacious and attractive person, but she had no way of earning a living. Maybe out of compassion, a friend of Kay's asked if she could rent the loft as a space to get married in. The friend suggested that she could bring in a caterer to take care of the food and service. Desperate to earn any money, Kay agreed. The wedding was a success and the caterer suggested that he'd be happy to rent the space again. After she rented it out several times, Kay realized that growing up in a family in which her parents were caterers had taught her a lot about the business. Even though she had never really worked for them, she had occasionally helped her folks as a teenager. She decided to try to cater a party herself. When it was successful, she started to develop the confidence to make this venture into an ongoing, and ultimately successful business.

A Brand New Start

Connie, who is a high school graduate, had four small children when she left her husband because he was physically abusive to her and the children.

Her husband disappeared, moving from state to state, and no amount of legal pursuit succeeded in getting the child support Connie desperately needed, even though the courts continually supported her right to child support and alimony in every state she sued him in. Her parents refused to assist her and the children in any way. They were deeply religious and felt that, despite the abuse, a marital separation was unconscionable. Her husband was part of a fundamentalist sect, as were her parents. She became increasingly frightened because the sect was known to kidnap children from women who abandoned the sect.

She took the children and left the state without telling anyone where she was going and moved a couple of thousand miles away. Completely on her own in a new community, she found a job driving a taxi and located day care for her children. Within six months, she took a Civil Service exam, did well, and got a job in the Social Security Administration. Connie did not make as much money as her ex-husband had, but for the first time in her life Connie knew real freedom. Her life was not stress-free, but she no longer had to fear the strict religious dictates of her husband and her parents that she did not share, or fear her husband's unpredictable violent attacks. In time, she remarried and she and her children regained their middle-class lifestyle.

Starting from the Bottom

Mary left her husband, an attorney, because she felt she could not go on living under his dictatorial rule. Her husband vowed to fight her for custody of the children. He agreed to a divorce only on the condition that she give him custody of their two children, ages eleven and thirteen. She would have liberal visitation rights with them and live nearby. This was drastic, but she was desperate, and accepted his terms. Mary had never worked, although she was in her late thirties.

After separating, she applied to the local manufacturing company and got a job in Human Resources. She is bright and articulate and has a pleasant personality. The job fit her very well. Her standard of living declined, but she was only supporting herself, so her modest income was adequate. She was greatly relieved to be away from her former husband.

Mary took advantage of various training and educational programs that the company offered, worked long hours, and got promoted several times. She maintained positive relationships with each of her children, even though her former husband never spoke to her again. She also eventually remarried, this time to an engineer. He had no children and took an active interest in hers. Once she remarried, between their joint incomes, she returned to her former comfortable lifestyle.

Making a Solid Commitment

When Patti Ann's husband left her, her two children were teenagers. He left her the house they lived in, which had a large mortgage, and he gave her some alimony and child support. Together, it was barely enough to get by on. In the last few years of her marriage, Patti Ann had worked intermittently as a real estate agent, trying to sell houses in her community, but with only limited success.

Once she was on her own, she tried to manage with her new financial limitations, but found herself very constrained, and anxious. She had no financial cushion. She needed expensive repairs to her house, but she couldn't afford them; she couldn't afford to do anything but pay her mortgage, feed and clothe her children and herself, and put gas in her car. Her parents were sympathetic, but had only a very limited ability to help her. She had taught elementary school before her marriage and the only other thing she knew how to do, or was prepared for, was selling real estate. So she got very serious about earning money. Within a few months, she had found a position teaching in a preschool part time and also rededicated herself to selling real estate. Shortly thereafter, she sold one house, then another, and gradually, developed a reasonably successful career for herself. She felt great satisfaction that she had risen to the challenge, that she had faced and was able to meet her financial obligations, and was stimulated by the work she was doing.

Transforming Your Life

Liz and her husband of seven years divorced when it came to light that he was an active homosexual, and he moved out to live with another man. They had no children. They had met in college, where they both got degrees as schoolteachers. After the separation, Liz found that living on her small teaching salary—and the isolation of living in a rural school district where she was teaching—offered her little. She applied for student loans and for entrance into a graduate business program in a large city. She was accepted for both. Two years later, after graduation,

Liz landed a well-paying job in a management-training program in a large department store chain. She stayed in the job successfully for a number of years, and met her second husband there. He was a supplier to the department store chain.

Paying for Guilt

We also interviewed several well-educated, middle-class women who felt so guilty for ending their marriages that they settled for permanent financial hardship for themselves. Margaret and her husband broke up when he found out she was having an affair. When the marriage ended, Margaret got custody of their two children. Out of guilt, fear, and poor legal advice, she foolishly agreed to a financial arrangement that reduced her and her children's standard of living drastically, despite the fact that her husband was a well-paid accountant. Margaret, who had never worked before, decided to go back to school to get skills to earn a living. She chose to become a teacher but, after graduation, she went to work in a very low-paying school district. Margaret never attempted to get a better-paying job. She never sought a new mate, although she is an attractive and personable woman. In fact, she put on a great deal of weight and made herself much less attractive.

More than a decade later, although Margaret's ex-husband and his second wife are very well off and her children are grown and out of the house, Margaret is still single and continues to eke out a meager living. She told us that her elderly father is affluent, but Margaret doesn't seek any assistance from him. Her children are doing well, but she would never ask them for any help, either. It is as if Margaret feels that once you screw up, you should keep paying for it for the rest of your life. "Divorce impoverishes women," she told us. While the statistics don't bear that out, that is what Margaret expected, and that is what she accepted.

Increasing Your Income

Other than a few high-profile "gold diggers," no one ever talks about the significant number of women, mostly those who have already been working, who become more affluent through divorce as a result of the combination of their own salaries, tax-free child support, alimony, and generous property settlements awarded by the courts.

Sara Beth and Wade each work full time. In their divorce settlement,

Wade had to provide substantial child support for their two adolescent daughters, who live mostly with Sara Beth. Since the couple's primary asset was their home, Wade had to sell his share of the house to Sara Beth in order to take any assets out of the marriage. Sara Beth and her attorney managed to negotiate a highly favorable price for the buyout of the house. Because of a drop in interest rates, Sara Beth refinanced the mortgage at a lower rate, and even rented out a small apartment in the basement of the house. After the separation, Sara Beth also got more serious about her career as a hair stylist in her own small shop. She felt that it was important to increase her fees and step up her marketing. As a result, three years later, her income has climbed quite a bit. Additionally, Sara Beth's boyfriend moved in and is sharing the expenses on the house. Sara Beth is living on a much increased income since she and Wade split up. Our interviews made us realize that this is not an uncommon situation, especially for middle-class women who divorce.

We should not feel too sorry for Wade. While his assets have diminished, his income during these three years has also increased significantly through his hard work and remarriage. We anticipate that because of this he will rebuild his assets. The research from Southern Methodist University by Kathleen O'Connell-Corcoran and our own interviews show that this is not unusual either. Most men who pay child support, but especially, men who are in service-sector or professional jobs, often register gains in their incomes in the years after the chaotic transition period following a divorce. This may be due to reduced distractions and an increased ability to focus on work as well as the increased energy supplied through forming new relationships and new families and the need to generate money to sustain their lifestyle and their numerous obligations.

In making a decision as to whether you should stay or go, we are trying to help you clear the fog. Don't let fears about money, about your children, about being alone, or your concern about other people's reactions to your separating cloud your judgment or paralyze you. If you stay, stay because you sincerely want to commit and dedicate yourself to making your marriage better, to working it out with this other worthwhile human being, and not just accepting the present unhappy status quo. Stay because you have hope that your spouse will join you in this effort.

Getting Legal Advice

Women and men who receive little or poor-quality legal advice risk accepting inequitable financial settlements. Some women we spoke with had not gotten their own attorneys, but mistakenly had agreed to use their husband's. We are not saying this can never work, but you need to know who you are dealing with. Is your spouse someone who will not try to take advantage of you? Is he or she fair? How angry is he or she? Divorce mediation can be a viable option if you and your spouse have the potential to agree on a financial settlement, living arrangements, and child custody and visitation issues. For many couples, this can work and save a lot of money, but it is clearly not for everyone.

If you decide to go, don't expect a fight, and don't look for one. In study after study, for example, Abigail Stewart's study of 160 families in the Greater Boston area and divorce records of 46,000 divorces in Brinig and Allen's survey of the divorce records in Connecticut, Virginia, Montana, and Oregon, published in 2000, at least 85 percent of divorce cases are settled out of court. This substantiates the assertion that the vast majority of separations and divorces are not contentious and are settled amicably. This is especially beneficial for children.

If you decide to separate, it is important to project your financial needs at least five years into the future before accepting a financial settlement. Seek legal counsel early in your decision-making process. This is very important. Consulting a matrimonial attorney doesn't commit you to any particular course of action. It is confidential and will help you to understand your financial, legal, and custodial options better, identify other options, and, hopefully, protect you against making serious misjudgments.

For men and women, separation is not a good time to be motivated by guilt or rage, although it is extremely hard not to be. We recommend that people pick an attorney who will complement their own personality. If you need a protector, you may need an attorney who is more aggressive than you are. On the other hand, if you need to curtail your aggression, seek an attorney who is a mediator and a negotiator. We also advise you to be guided by how aggressive your spouse is and your spouse's attorney is.

The Role of Poverty

Whether you are a man or a woman, if money problems plague you and your spouse, you need to understand how powerfully this is contributing to your marital problems. Poverty and financial stress are among the major causes of marital problems and divorce. While divorcing does strain finances, the deterioration of a marriage very often begins with financial reverses. These reverses can be caused by unemployment, underemployment, and the erosion of income because of inflation. In our interviews, men from divorcing families frequently attribute their divorces to chronic arguments with their wives about lack of money. Any drop in income creates hardship for a couple. While this is true for people living at or near the poverty line, it is also true for more affluent couples whose lifestyle is affected by a significant drop in income.

Downturns in the economy, like the financial crisis beginning in 2008, occur cyclically and the information revolution continues to displace people. Men and women who have little employment experience or out-of-date education and skills fall further and further behind. In his book *American Fiscal Policy,* Nobel Prize–winning economist Lester Thurow states: "The traditional family is being destroyed . . . by a modern economic system that is not congruent with family values. Besides [unemployment and] falling wages America's other . . . problems pale into insignificance. [Poorer] men have a strong economic incentive to bail out of family responsibilities."

Perils of Income Volatility

A 2007 study by economist John Nunley at Middle Tennessee State University's Department of Economics and Finance examined the impact of income volatility on marriage stability. Not surprisingly, he concluded that negative shocks to family income increase the likelihood that both men and women will initiate divorce. More of a surprise was that he found that positive shocks—that is, sudden gains in income; for example, from a large bonus or promotion—also increase the likelihood of divorce, but only those initiated by men. In order to know if it's time to go, you should consider whether your family's finances have changed recently. If they have, your relationship itself may be less of the problem, and the financial stress you two are coping with may be much more of the problem.

The rate of divorce reached its peak in 1981 at over 50 percent, and has gradually declined to about 40 percent since then, leveling off in the last few years. This is particularly true for middle-income families. Among poor people, the divorce rate has not leveled off, but has continued to increase.

If a man loses his job, the probability of his divorcing more than doubles. The likelihood of divorce grows even worse if both spouses are unemployed.

The rate of marriage among poor people has also declined in this period. Poor people are more than twice as likely to divorce as middle-income people. This is true across all racial and ethnic groups.

If you and your spouse have experienced economic hardship, one or both of you have lost your job, or your income has been reduced, recognize the central role this is playing in your marital discord. Remember that economic cycles, and bad luck, may be temporary, not, hopefully, lasting a lifetime. The bleak picture you may be facing right now is just as likely in time to get better, as it is to stay the same or get worse. So to answer the question of how do you know if it's time to go, you should ask yourself whether the trouble you are currently experiencing in your marriage is only about the financial difficulties you are currently experiencing, which may only be temporary, or whether you have been glossing over deep differences between you and your spouse because your finances were sufficiently robust in the past to allow you to ignore those differences.

Women's Working Helps Marriages

If a family has enough income, from the husband's or the wife's work, or both, it minimizes a major source of marital tension. This includes the 25 percent of marriages where women earn more money than their husbands.

Rather than reducing women's marital satisfaction, outside employment generally increases it.

This is not to say that a two-career household doesn't put stress on a marriage and the people in it. Of course it does. But the financial benefits, and the increased self-esteem for both people are more often beneficial to the quality and longevity of the marriage.

If you are a woman who is not currently working, and you are considering whether it is time to go, you may want to consider becoming employed. The increased income will be useful, possibly taking some financial pressure off your husband, but your increased sense of independence and the stimulation you'll derive may also lift your spirits, which may reduce some of the tension in your marriage. If, ultimately, you do decide to go, the independent income, the network of contacts, and the feeling of competence in navigating the outside world will all help you in making your way in a new situation.

Questions to Think About

1. Am I using fear of financial hardship as an excuse for staying in my marriage because of other fears that are harder to think about? Yes___No___

2. Am I young enough to feel that I can make a new beginning, finish or extend my education, build or start my career? Or am I old enough so that I have built a career and saved some money so I have a safety net? Yes___No___

3. Am I prepared to make some financial sacrifices if I need to? Yes___No___

4. Can I tolerate a dispute over money, if my spouse forces one? Yes___No___

5. Are there enough assets so that each of us will be able to go forward and manage? Yes___No___

6. Can I generate some alternative child care if I need to work? Yes___No___

7. Is there anyone else whom I could share expenses with or get help from if I divorce? Yes___No___

8. Could I increase my energy and commitment to my career or work so I could potentially increase my earnings? Yes___No___

9. Has my marriage suffered because of a significant change in my family's finances, either down or up? Yes___No___

CHAPTER 16

The Real Damage

In previous chapters, we tried to diminish your concerns, but realistically you need to recognize that if you decide to separate, divorce is a trade-off and you will pay a price. Divorce causes loss, disruption, and sometimes incurs stigma and discrimination. At the end of a marriage there is frustration—the frustration of not being able to make it work and not being able to persuade your partner to change. You are likely to feel angry at yourself as well as your partner because of this powerlessness. Here is what people told us about their negative experiences. We present them in their own words, as they told them to us. We don't necessarily agree with everything that each person says, but we include their varied comments here because we believe some will resonate with each of our readers. It may be useful to you to hear directly from others about their experiences of loss, disruption, revenge, and conflicts over visitation or property. When you are afraid of something, sizing up your fears helps you get a more realistic handle on them and helps you to face them. Perhaps these people's accounts can help you by speaking directly to you about the saddest part of their personal experiences of divorce from the vantage point of having it years in the past.

Loss

Russell:

> When I divorced, I experienced many losses, not just one. I lost my family; I lost the person I had once loved, and, in some ways, still do—the mother of my children. I lost everyday contact with my children because my ex and I share custody. Although, I have to admit, in retrospect—and I feel sheepish telling you this—there is a silver lining that people don't generally

talk about. Once I got used to the new situation with the kids, it hasn't been as bad as I expected it to be. If anything, I am now a little closer to them, although it took some time, and I find my time away from them gives me a chance to unwind and get personal things done. I'm not sure, but I think that my ex-wife feels the same way.

When I divorced, I lost my household, my neighbors, and some friends. I lost some relatives—a few of them I don't miss, but some I loved, and I do miss them. I've had some decline in my standard of living. I'm in a decent apartment now. I used to live in a beautiful house.

One of my biggest losses, one that makes me feel guilty, is my children's loss of their sense of stability and confidence that all is right with the world. They are not so innocent anymore.

I lost my sexual partner, but I found a new one. I feel like I am describing the Lost & Found Department in a museum. I lost my companion, who had long ago stopped being my friend. Many of these things were gone a long time ago, or never existed, except in my imagination. It hit me, all at once, like a bombshell. But, in hindsight that's not the way it really happened.

Jeremy:

I've been divorced four years. My older son is okay. He's married. He never seemed deeply affected by our divorce. But I have a lot of uncertainty about my younger son. I wonder if I have contributed to his problems. I have regrets about him. He's nineteen. He's already been in two serious car accidents. The second one both my son and the driver of the other car were nearly killed. Maybe he is pulling himself together. Now he's in AA, and he's a full-time college student.

My ex-wife's a nurse. She has a full social life, but I wish she was with someone. She and our sons don't know about my new woman. Sometimes I have dinner with my younger son and my ex-wife. It's cordial, but it's not friendly.

Madeline:

Maybe it was mostly an illusion, but living inside my marriage provided me with a sense of safety, respectability, and acceptance. My divorce shattered those feelings. My marriage provided me with a structure. Without it, I felt at sea for a long time. Our normal routines were gone. I no longer had the expectation of my husband coming home at the end of the day, although I was so glad my children lived with me because they gave my life a sense of meaning and shape. They say people who have custody of their kids have it easier. I think that was true for me. One of the greatest losses is not being able to parent our children together. No one can love your children as much as you and their father do. No one can be as interested. You want to be able to talk with their father about the good and the bad things going on for them, but you can't. Our daughter got married recently and we both made her wedding. It was great that we could do this together after all these years, and get along while doing it. I know it meant a great deal to our daughter.

I believe children of divorced parents have a lifelong sadness. It doesn't mean they think their parents should have stayed together, although my kids voiced that on and off for years, especially when they were young. It's a sadness that the dream of a happy family, one created by their parents, was unrealized. It's almost like unrequited love. It's as if my children retain a vision of a happy family, a vision that we could not deliver on. As long as their father and I were together, my children believed that the world, which was their family, was a perfect place. But it wasn't.

Then there is the never-ending awkwardness of holidays—my year, your year, and inflicting all those new relatives on them. Both my ex and I have remarried. It works out, but it isn't the Norman Rockwell Thanksgiving painting that we all hold somewhere in our minds.

Rebecca:

My [second] husband and I went to a party last night. We were the only couple among five couples who had been divorced and were in a second marriage. I felt envious of the history the others had with one another. They had continuity. There are so many years that Ethan and I didn't spend together. Maybe the most important thing is that we don't have children together. Children, to a great extent, make a marriage. Without children in common, you focus more on each other.

It's hard to be a stepparent. Ethan and I don't really see eye to eye about parenting. You have a better chance of working together if you are the real parents. You can't feel the same way if you are not the parent. I feel left out when Ethan's children tell him things, and he doesn't think to tell me. Maybe he thinks I wouldn't be interested. We sometimes visit with our own children separately.

When you divorce, your children always have some anger. In many divorces the kids have been protected from the parents' conflict. Even if they've sensed that something was wrong, they were still protected. When you break up, they have the feeling that they can't trust you anymore. After all, I left their father.

Matt:

Divorce is like a death. I think it would be hard, but it would be better, if divorced couples didn't feel they were breaking off their relationship entirely, at least for their children's sake, but for our own as well. It would be better if there was some basis of contact that could be maintained. It would be better for the kids. But I guess it's easier if the break is complete. There should be more scope for an amicable divorce.

Being in a second marriage is not like being in a first. Sometimes I'll look at a photograph, or remember an event, and I have to ask myself, "Who did I go through this with?" I can't always remember which of my two wives shared that part of my life. It's confusing. It's also a little sad, and honestly, a little funny.

For the first few years after I remarried, my son, who is very close to me, dealt with my second wife like she was a foreign object. He wouldn't even look at her. When his mom and I were breaking up, he was eleven. He said to me, "This is unacceptable. Fix it." He was fed up with our fighting. I said, "It's not possible." The divorce left me feeling very guilty.

Disruption

Fortunately, a majority of divorces are not highly antagonistic. Stewart in her Boston study, as well as others, have found that the vast majority of divorcing people come to mutually agreed on solutions over child custody, finances, and living arrangements. That's very welcome news because ongoing conflict with your ex, sometimes including revenge and retaliation, causes serious, lasting, if not permanent, damage to everyone in the family. In our opinion, the measure of disruption is directly related to the amount of conflict that one or both of you create. Usually, this kind of disruption involves disagreements about the children and property, but also attacks on each other's reputation.

When conflict between parents during a separation is high, children's behavior is likely to deteriorate. Parents faced with this deteriorating behavior are more easily frustrated with the children and less able to cope. One recent study showed an increased rate of child abuse in single-parent families.

Conflict over Visitation

Ryan, a teacher we interviewed, described how his former wife, Kristen, consistently wedges herself between him and their twelve-year-old son. "I'm supposed to have Kevin every other Thanksgiving, Christmas, and Easter. I haven't had Kevin with me on Christmas for the last three years, two of which were my years.

"Kristen has a sister in California, near Disneyland, who we almost never saw or visited in our twelve years of marriage. Kristen has decided to go to California for Christmas for the last three years. Without consulting me, she tells Kevin he's invited to come with her if he wants to, and she'll get the tickets. She usually does this in the previous spring, long before I have made any plans for the holiday. Besides, I tend to spend the holiday locally with my family. I can't compete with Disneyland, and yet Kristen keeps offering this temptation to Kevin, which is very hard for a twelve-year-old to turn down. Last spring Kevin graduated from middle school. Although I asked him about it, I never got notice of the date of the graduation, or got an invitation to it until I found out three days before, and by then it was too late for me to arrange to be there. Anyway, I felt I wasn't wanted. Kristen went with her boyfriend."

As we questioned Ryan, it emerged that in the last few years of their marriage, as it deteriorated, Kristen had formed a more and more powerful bond with Kevin, one that made Ryan feel increasingly excluded. She belittled Ryan in front of Kevin, and criticized Ryan's family. This has continued into their separation and divorce and has undermined Kevin's motivation to spend time with his father. Kevin probably feels as if he is betraying his mother when he spends time with, or has a good time with, his dad.

When a mother or father consistently undermines the relationship between the child and the other parent, it hurts the undermined parent, but it is likely to create lasting damage for the child and the child's relationship with both parents.

Two thousand years ago, Sophocles wrote a play about Medea, who killed her children, whom she claimed she loved. She killed them to punish her husband, their father, Jason. He had left Medea for another woman. Judith Wallerstein calls the destructive undermining of the other parent's relationship with the child the "Medea Syndrome," after that character. We feel that it is equally prevalent among both men and women. No one is perfect, and most people who are considering divorce feel the temptation at times to use their children to frustrate or upset a difficult spouse. Please resist it.

We can't overstate the negative effects on children of losing touch entirely with their fathers. One patient of Dr. Birnbach's, whose father abandoned the family when the patient was already eighteen years old, is still devastated at age forty that his dad will not respond to attempts at contact. What we have seen in children of divorce is a variety of possible consequences. Some men whose dads were driven away, or fled, seem to have trouble forming intimate relationships, which may lead to their increased risk of adultery and multiple marriages. Nick told us that his father abandoned the family when he was five and he was raised entirely by his mother and her second husband. Nick was never faithful to his first wife and she eventually divorced him. Now, in his second marriage, he confesses that he still has the same desire to stray, but "Now I know the right thing to do to be a good husband, and I want to do the right thing."

A strong relationship with one parent can serve as a powerful protector for a child's future development if the other parent drops out. You'll recall that if the relationship is with the same-sex parent, it seems to be an even better guarantee. This is evidenced in the women we interviewed who grew up in households where the father had deserted entirely. Where the relationship with the mother was strong and wholesome, the girl fared well—both in her own marriage and her own career. Where the relationship with the mother was more troubled, the girl often fared poorly in both areas.

Revenge against Property

Sometimes divorce disruption causes one of the two of you to take revenge against property. Everyone has heard horror stories about the revenge some people take in very acrimonious divorces—it even makes headlines. Paul bitterly told us that he believes his wife reported to the IRS that he was evading paying some income tax. Six months after his separation, he was audited for the first time in his life. The IRS found that he owed thousands of dollars. Unfortunately, Paul doesn't have any money because he had exhausted all his savings to pay his divorce attorney. The IRS was not sympathetic, and he is obligated to turn over to the government not only what he owes in taxes but also large penalties and interest, which grows month by month. This is in addition to Paul's having to pay alimony and child support. He believes he will be in debt for many years to come. While we in no way endorse tax evasion, and the IRS might have audited Paul anyway, still, Paul's children in no way benefited from the serious financial impact that resulted from the audit, as well as the stress that it put on Paul. It also fueled his ongoing anger at his former wife.

Jamal told us that his wife charged thousands of dollars on each of several credit cards shortly before she asked him to leave the house. In his divorce proceedings, his wife reported that Jamal supposedly had a secret stock market portfolio, amounting to many thousands of dollars, although he earns a modest income and his wife doesn't work. Jamal paid his lawyer handsomely to prove to the judge that his portfolio was actually an imaginary account that he had devised as a game he played with himself on the computer to see how he would do in the stock market if he did have any money to invest. It was a game his professor had taught the students to play in an economics course he took in college. Jamal is still paying off the credit card debt and alimony to his wife, who has no children at home but who refuses to work.

Diana never knew that everything was in her husband's name until it was too late. She didn't know what their assets were, or where they were. It had never been important to her. After he left her, she tried to get him to relinquish a fair share of the family's assets that she was entitled to. He hired top attorneys and because he had all the money, he used every legal maneuver to extend and drag out the divorce proceedings. When a judge eventually awarded her a modest settlement, her husband appealed. He declared bankruptcy after he moved to Florida, where he continues to live a luxurious life. He just wore Diana out. She gave up.

When they divorced, Stephanie got the house and George got the country cabin. Six months after their divorce, the country place mysteriously had an electrical fire and burned to the ground. The insurance company investigated what they felt were suspicious circumstances, but they were unable to prove arson. George was underinsured, and, when he eventually got the insurance settlement, he sold the land because the settlement was not nearly enough money to rebuild the house.

It's natural to have fantasies of revenge when you feel you have been mistreated by your partner. But if you decide it is time to go, we urge you not to act on them. Especially if you have children together, remember that this other person will continue to be your children's mother or father for the rest of her or his life. Your children can't get another biological parent. At best, a stepparent can be a great joy and comfort, but a stepparent is not ever the same for your children as their real parents.

Reputation Busting

Disruption also comes in the form of destroying relationships and careers. We heard from Max that his ex-wife called his boss and told him that Max was having an affair with a colleague. Max's boss confronted him, and within weeks both Max and the colleague were forced to leave the firm.

In another case, a few years after her acrimonious divorce, Lindsay ran into her old next-door neighbor. In talking together, the neighbor was surprised to learn that the neighborhood gossip, apparently fueled by Lindsay's ex-husband, was that Lindsay had broken up someone else's marriage and run off with the man to Mexico. In truth, Lindsay was living alone a few towns away. She had, in fact, dated a single man who was Mexican.

The most awful attack on reputation that can occur, albeit very infrequently, is when one spouse tries to get leverage in custody, financial, or visitation negotiations by accusing the other of physical and/or sexual abuse of the children. In the one case we came upon during our interviews, the accusation of physical abuse of a child was investigated by a court-appointed psychiatrist, who noted in his detailed report that the accusation could not be substantiated. In this case, the unsubstantiated accusation created enormous bitterness that prolonged the divorce struggles and consumed a huge amount of money. Of course, if you believe that your spouse is physically or sexually abusing your child, you should report this to the authorities immediately.

Stigma

Living with the stigma, real or imagined, that continues to be attached to divorce is another consequence you'll face. Divorced men and women sometimes feel they and their children are excluded by their community, friends, and family, especially in communities and families where there is not a high incidence of divorce. People who are separating and divorcing tend to be extremely sensitive, but they also need to be thoughtful about whether they are being overly sensitive to feelings of being criticized and excluded.

Three years after his divorce, Carlos and his girlfriend were attending a soccer game that Carlos's ten-year-old daughter was playing in. After the game, a group of parents and children went to the local pizza shop. The kids sat at one big table, the parents sat at another. After seating his daughter with the other kids, Carlos automatically sat alone with his girlfriend instead of joining his former neighbors at the parents' table. He felt that his former neighbors had not been encouraging him to join them. After Carlos ordered a pizza, one of his former women neighbors came over and said, "You should have joined us. You would have been welcome." Carlos still felt guilty that he had wanted the divorce, and he felt doubly guilty that he was with a new woman, not his former wife, who was still friends with many of these neighbors, so he had assumed they would have preferred to eat without him. Carlos's girlfriend told him later that, in her opinion, the invitation to join his neighbors was genuine, and that they should have.

Newly divorced women and men often point out that much of their former social life is lost because it is a "couples' world." They explain that sometimes former friends fear them as potential rivals for their mates. Felicia told us that she found out years later, after she had remarried, that married women friends didn't want to invite her over when she was newly divorced. Felicia was attractive and flirtatious and the other women didn't want her around their husbands even though she and her husband had been popular with the same group when they were together.

How the stigma of divorce operates in the professional and business world was brought to light in an interview with an engineering professor from a major university. He described why he was afraid to let colleagues know he was divorcing. "I was sitting on a committee with fellow department members. We were awarding graduate scholarships. Another professor objected to a candidate someone recommended. 'We can't give him a scholarship, he's not stable. He's divorced.'"

If you decide that it's time to go, you need to overcome your shame and, as we've said earlier, get your version of the reasons for the breakdown of your marriage—a sympathetic version—out to family and friends quickly. People tend to be judgmental and take sides. If they have only one version of a story to go by, they are likely to believe it.

Above all, get good legal guidance. Once you've made your decision, be open with your friends and relatives about your side of the story. Speaking with the right people about your desire to separate will help you to face your fears. You'll get support and some good ideas about how to manage your situation. They are also likely to help you feel more courageous. Above all, avoid getting into arguments with your mate if it's at all possible, and please resist the temptation to tell your children just one side of the story.

Questions to Think About

1. Am I prepared to give up this person I once loved?
   Yes___No___

2. Am I prepared to share custody of my children and not see them every day? Yes___No___

3. Am I prepared to give up some of the current structure of my life, and some of my normal routines, even some friends and relatives? Yes___No___

4. Am I prepared for my husband/wife to give me a difficult time when it comes to child-rearing values and/or visitation?
   Yes___No___

5. Am I prepared to possibly face bitterness or retaliation from my ex if I divorce? Yes___No___

6. Can I handle life in a "couples' world" and build a network of support without my mate? Yes___No___

7. Can I get past feelings of failure or shame if I divorce?
   Yes___No___

Part Four

Knowing When It's Time to Go

CHAPTER 17

Rescued Marriages: Exhausting Every Remedy

Step 9: Take another inventory—
Have I exhausted every remedy to heal my marriage?
Do I have any realistic hope? What am I waiting for?

For most people, divorce is not a logical decision; it is an emotional decision. You may ask yourself, will divorce be financially costly? Of course it will. Would my children prefer for our family to stay together? Very likely, yes. Would our friends and relatives be happier? Probably yes. If I divorce, will it cause me disruption and anxiety? Undoubtedly yes. These are not the reasons people should stay together or divorce. Considerations of money, children's, relatives', and friends' wishes, and concerns about the disruption to family life ultimately should not be the reasons why you do or do not divorce.

It may be helpful for you to know why most men and women say they separated and divorced. This should help you gain some perspective on your own decision. Abigail Stewart found that three-quarters of both the men and women she interviewed for her book *Separating Together* said they divorced because they found specific behaviors of their spouse intolerable. Among them: a partner who is chronically disrespectful and unsupportive or a partner who spends much too much time—evenings or weekends—out alone, or with friends, away from the family, demonstrating that he or she is not sufficiently committed to family life or to his or her responsibilities as a husband or wife. Most people in the study mentioned that several problems finally led them to divorce, not just one. In addition to intolerable behavior, other commonly mentioned problems were:

- growing apart, having different values
- the partner's inflexibility, including with respect to gender roles

- the partner's immaturity
- the partner's extramarital affairs
- the couple's differences over money
- the couple's conflicts in terms of child rearing
- behavior problems of the spouse, such as alcoholism and/or drug abuse
- emotional abuse

Deciding to get a divorce means believing your life can be better. There isn't necessarily a logical proof of this; it's a belief.

Physical violence of the spouse was mentioned by almost one out of four women, but rarely by men. Most people reported that they came to the decision to divorce gradually and only after years of trying to persuade their partner to change in the areas that were driving them apart. No one in the study took the decision to divorce lightly.

You should only decide it is time to go if you have lost all hope. Losing all hope means you have come to the decision, as the people in this study did, that your partner is never going to change in the ways that you need him to, that you are not going to change in the ways he needs you to, and that the current status quo has worn you down and frustrated you to the point where the emotional price you and your children are paying outweighs more practical considerations, such as temporary financial and other life disruptions that often accompany divorce.

Before you make the decision to go, you want to assure yourself that you have exhausted every remedy. Now is the time to tell your spouse just how bad things are. Don't be afraid to cause conflict in hopes of making things better between the two of you. A vow of silence, never speaking about these things, will ensure that the problems only get worse. Your spouse may get furious when you bring up some aspect of her behavior that is driving you away, but now is not the time to back off. Now is the time to fight for the relationship—literally. If you intentionally cause conflict with the idea of bringing a certain problem to a head so that it can be resolved, you are on solid ground.

The following ten questions may help you and your spouse break through the problems that divide you. You will see that these remedies did provide help for the couples whose marriages we describe, couples who rescued their marriages and brought them back from the brink. The remedies require change on your part, as well as your spouse's. It bears repeating that the truth in disputes between couples most often lies in the middle, and that the problems couples experience are a result of the interaction between them, not just the actions of one or the other person. Typically, each member of the couple is unmotivated to respond to the other person's requests because of their frustrations in the marriage. Each is waiting for the other to make the first move. That's why, to stay happy enough in the marriage, each of you has to be willing to make changes. We are asking you to start a dialogue with one another on a level that you probably have rarely touched before. We feel this dialogue is essential before you make such an important decision as to whether it is time to go.

1. Have I let my spouse know how serious my level of discontent is and that I am close to a breaking point, close to a divorce?

Many spouses find it inconceivable that their partner would divorce them. Your partner may see you as all bark, but no bite. Until your partner knows how serious you are, that you really will leave him if things continue as they are, until he really gets it, you don't have much leverage to motivate change. Tell your partner how serious you are. Don't be afraid to "fight for the relationship."

Speaking up doesn't mean giving your partner a laundry list of your complaints. This is only likely to alienate him further. "You always . . ." and "You never . . ." are harsh, sweeping judgments that are likely to make your partner defensive. Pick one thing to talk about, something that you believe your partner could work on, and might agree to under the right circumstances.

Most issues have two sides. Seeking a negotiated agreement, in which each of you gives something of importance to the other, is likely to create an enduring and motivated solution.

No matter how distasteful it may seem to you, accept that at least some of what your spouse is saying to you is accurate. If you give some, you are more likely to get something back.

Emily is doing that and seems to be succeeding. Her husband has said that she doesn't stand up to him enough. It was true, and he was getting more and more disrespectful toward her as a result. Lately she makes him deliver on his agreement with her to clean up the dishes at the end of a meal, not leave them until the next day, which drives her crazy. She insists that he spend time with her if she goes with him to one of his business functions. She has spent years sulking after standing around watching him flirt with his vendors and leaving her to her own devices in situations where she hardly knows a soul. Now she doesn't sulk; she fights back. Part of him doesn't like what she is doing. He gets angry at her, but she reminds him that this was what he said he wanted—for her to stand up to him more. She has upset the status quo. Sometimes, she says, they are now closer than ever. Sometimes they are hardly talking, but she finally has hope, because she meant it when she said that if things didn't change, she was going to leave. He grasps the seriousness of her intent, and he's responding.

2. Have I tried self-improvement that would matter to my spouse? Have I tried going along with some of my spouse's insistent requests of me?

We spoke earlier about delayed compliance. Many times our spouse is the first person to identify an area of our behavior that really needs to change. Usually, we resist this furiously, because who wants to admit that some aspect of our behavior needs modification? It is especially difficult to accept this feedback if we are already having difficulties in our marriage. If we can listen and commit to working on changing, it can save a marriage. It's a pity that people so often make these changes only after a divorce. Perhaps the divorce would not have been necessary if the change had come sooner.

Shawn's wife, Andrea, was never fond of him being a "control freak," but it really came to a head after they had their little boy. As far as she was concerned, it was ridiculous that he was micromanaging every move she made with the baby—how to hold him, how to nurse him, how to fasten the diaper properly, how to burp him, how to put him to sleep. Shawn had already had some of these control issues at work with colleagues and subordinates, so he knew this was a tendency of his. After he and Andrea repeatedly argued about his interference, she started to withdraw from him. In therapy, he was able to accept that he was alienating and undermining his wife, a new mother, whom he loved. He started working hard to change. He learned to keep his mouth shut and let her be the expert most of the time. Their arguing declined dramatically.

Drew and Ilene were going through a very rough patch in their marriage. Ilene found a lot of Drew's behavior toward his career, and toward life in general, too passive. One symptom of Drew's passivity was his almost daily use of marijuana. He'd come home from work and no matter what else was going on, he'd have to first smoke. To Ilene, smoking marijuana made

Drew remote and even more passive. Instead of talking about all her feelings about Drew's passivity, Ilene singled out the marijuana issue to address. It wasn't easy. She anticipated that he'd be defensive and angry, which he was. In several very frank, sometimes heated, discussions, spread over a couple of months, she said that the remoteness she felt when he smoked was hurtful to her and that it made her feel lonely and uncared for.

Drew protested that Ilene was doing things that made him feel lonely and uncared for as well. Specifically, she sometimes flirted with men, especially in social gatherings, but he thought at her job as well. What started as Ilene's gripe against Drew evolved into a negotiation. Although Ilene was initially defensive, she wisely realized that she was not blameless. With these kinds of issues, each member of the couple usually shares some of the responsibility. Most issues have two sides. Seeking a negotiated agreement in which each of you gives something of importance to the other is likely to create an enduring and motivated solution. Sadly, the first reaction of too many people is to defend themselves against any request for change from their mate rather than remaining open enough to at least weigh the potential benefits to the marriage of meeting the request. Both Drew and Ilene were doing things without realizing it was hurtful and upsetting to the other. Over time, first Drew agreed to give up his beloved marijuana. Gradually, Ilene became more and more careful about her behavior and her flirtations, reduced the frequency of her flirting, and ultimately stopped the behavior altogether.

3. Have we tried spending more time with each other? Have we tried spending less time with each other?

There is no blueprint for how much time a couple should spend together. Different people have very different needs. Don't be defensive about what you need. A problem arises when one person's need for companionship is quite different from his mate's. Even if your mate feels differently, you must speak up and express your needs. It's useful if you can also offer practical ideas about how to alleviate the problem from your point of view.

Evan told us that he and his wife were both very busy professionals and whatever time they had at home was spent with their children and on household responsibilities. They were drifting dangerously far apart. Someone at work told Evan about a whitewater canoe school where couples learn to canoe together—one in the front of the canoe, one in the back—down somewhat treacherous river rapids. His wife went along, although dubiously. Learning to work together to stay afloat was just what they needed. They decided they really enjoyed canoeing together, but more, spending time alone together. As a result, they added a regular date night and found it to be very helpful

Briana was really annoyed one Saturday morning because her parents were staying with them, the kids were home, and her husband just disappeared for hours. When he finally showed up around lunchtime, she was angry about his disappearing act. She hadn't even known where he was. She couldn't help but be moved when he explained to her that he felt suffocated by all the family they constantly had around, and that he never had any peace, or time alone—just work and the family. He had gone to the local Barnes & Noble store during those hours, bought a cup of coffee, and was reading. He loved it. She understood that spending less time together in this situation could bolster their marriage.

4. Have I taken steps to improve our sex life, if that is an issue?

When Ashley and Craig were first married, as you might imagine, they always went to bed at the same time. Two years later, after Ashley had a baby, she started going to bed early because she had to wake up in the middle of the night for a feeding, as well as get up very early in the morning for another one. Craig's schedule stayed more or less the same. He still had to get up at 7:30 in the morning to get ready for work. He still went to sleep at around 11:30 most nights. Even after the baby was sleeping through the night, Ashley continued to feel tired and go to bed by 9:30. Craig kept to his same schedule too. They fought increasingly. They also were both aware that the romance had gone out of their relationship. In talking it over, Craig brought up that Ashley was always sleeping by the time he got into bed, and that she was cranky if he tried to wake her up. She often complained that she wasn't getting enough sleep as it was.

After talking it over, they agreed that things might be better if they could figure out a way to go to bed at the same time and make efforts to rekindle the romantic aspect of their relationship. They tried various ways and ultimately settled on a mixture of times to go to bed, sometimes early to accommodate Ashley, sometimes later for Craig, and sometimes not at the same times at all. And they each made attempts in their own ways to put a spark in their sex life. It took time and persistence, but their fighting declined as their romance increased.

If the breakdown of sex in your marriage is more a cause than a result of the tremendous strain between you, you need professional help for your sexual problems. There are therapists who specialize in sexual problems and they are easy to find. Perhaps you should seek a referral from your family physician after he or she has ruled out physical causes of your sexual problems.

5. Have I tried getting a job to increase our income or to provide more stimulation in my life?

Natalie and Josh had three children and she helped him part time in his picture-framing business. The business was Josh's; he started it, and he loved it. For years Natalie helped out with sales, and she was good at it, but it didn't give her satisfaction. Natalie felt envious of Josh. She enjoyed raising their children when they were little, but now that they were in school full time, she felt unfulfilled. She blamed Josh for discouraging her from pursuing her own career. She had always enjoyed designing and making clothing for their children. She was so good at it that friends and relatives would sometimes ask her to make party dresses for their little girls, and children's clothing for other special occasions. A few times people had insisted that she take money for her efforts. Josh acted resentful when she took time away from the framing business, the kids, and him to follow this passion of hers, or take time for herself.

This made Natalie angry. She became less affectionate and less interested in sex with Josh. They argued often. Then Josh, who loves Natalie very much, became alarmed at the downhill slide in their marriage. He had an idea. For Christmas, he enrolled her in a course in fashion design at a well-known fashion training institute. She was thrilled. Natalie caught the teacher's attention with her designs, and he offered her an opportunity to work for him at his company as an assistant to the designer. It was for more money than she was earning with Josh. They talked it over and agreed that she should take it. She loved it. She would come home from work excited about what she was doing. By helping her to feel much more satisfied in her life, Josh made a wonderful investment in their marriage.

Mark was a highly paid executive when his company merged, and at age fifty-three he was given an early retirement. For the next eighteen months, Mark received his full salary, he didn't seriously look for work, and instead he and his wife, who does not work, enjoyed what amounted to a protracted second honeymoon. When Mark's severance pay ended, he found it hard to find a new job, partly because of his age. At the same time, his relationship with his wife began to deteriorate. They argued with increasing frequency and bitterness about many things, only one of which was his sporadic efforts to find a job. The financial stresses that they were gradually experiencing were causing them to become more irritable and argumentative with each other on many subjects. Mark eventually found a new job, though at only half his original salary, and that, combined with his pension from his former company, alleviated the financial pressure. Their marriage was able to recover, narrowly averting divorce.

Mel and Susan have never had a tranquil marriage. They have fought about many things over the years, and even talked on and off about separating, but never have done it. Susan was dissatisfied with Mel's earning capacity, even though she didn't work during the years she spent raising their two children. Of course, there are other issues in their marriage. For one thing, Susan resents Mel's withdrawn and cranky nature. After twenty-five years of marriage, when their children left for college, Susan, who was forty-seven at the time, went to work as an administrative assistant.

She enjoys the work; she is successful and receives a lot of praise, something she doesn't get much of from Mel. She also finds that the men and women she works with find her attractive, smart, and funny, qualities that Mel seldom remarks about. She is now sixty-five. Susan's career, which has continued for many years, hasn't created any miracles in her marriage, but neither has it done any harm. On the contrary, while "Mel is still Mel," she told us, she loves getting positive feedback, stimulation, and financial rewards, and it takes some of the pressure off her marriage. So she and Mel continue their lives together.

6. Have I tried stepping down from my career track or adjusting my ambitions?
When Keith started a small business with his friend Mike, they made a rapid success of it. They had a good idea; they were aggressive, took reasonable risks, and they were very hard workers. Spurred by their new affluence, they moved their young families into nice suburban homes, bought new expensive cars, and began living a much more luxurious life than any of them had ever known. When an economic downturn hit, the business

faltered. They were poorly capitalized and they resorted to an ill-advised and illegal deal with shady characters to try to rescue the business. It didn't work, and the two men wound up being criminally charged. As first-time offenders, Mike and Keith got suspended sentences and were fined. Both were also forced to declare bankruptcy.

As a result of the bankruptcy, Keith's family's standard of living plummeted; the car, the house, everything went through dramatic downsizing. This put severe strains on his marriage for several years. But Keith's marriage was a strong one. He and Heidi were high school sweethearts. They had two young children, and they saw eye to eye on most things. They had strong relationships with their extended family, which helped them to get through the tough time. Both of their families encouraged Keith to try another business venture when he got past his difficulties.

Mike's marriage, on the other hand, fell apart. It had never been a strong one. His wife, Marie, who told us this story, had strongly disapproved of her husband's partnership with Keith, and even more so, the way the partners handled their business difficulties. Marie's parents had always disapproved of Mike, and were upset to have their daughter's husband involved in criminal activity. During the successful years of the business, Marie explained that she had enjoyed the affluence and the excitement of the economic ride up. Mike had looked pretty good to her in that light. She confessed that she had buried the strong value differences that separated them. But when their standard of living declined following the bankruptcy, she could no longer gloss over their differences. She was furious with him for dragging her into this situation, and she left him soon after.

What happened to Keith and Heidi and Mike and Marie is typical of what Jonathan Fisher from the U.S. Bureau of Labor Statistics and Angela Lyons from the University of Illinois report in their study of bankruptcy and divorce during the years 1991–1995. The two are causally related. Bankruptcy increases the likelihood of divorce. It is also true that divorce increases the likelihood of bankruptcy.

7. Have I talked to family and friends who are likely to be objective and neutral to get their perspective?

This happened to us. Tammy and Avi, dear friends, were having trouble in their marriage, but neither of them spoke about it, either to one another, or to anyone else. Certainly, they had not spoken about it to us, although we suspected there was increased tension between them. One Saturday they told us they had argued on and off all day before coming to our house for dinner. When they arrived, the strain between them was obvious. At some point, one of us said, "What's going on between you two?" because they were quiet and edgy. Tammy blurted out, "I can't stand what Avi's wearing. He won't work with me on anything. He's so stubborn. Look at how fat he has gotten again!" Avi was angered and humiliated by her public attack. He retaliated by calling her a control freak, and he threatened to reveal some deep dark secret about her to us, which silenced her momentarily. The atmosphere between them was thick with hostility.

To try to be helpful, we started talking with them about times in our marriage when we had hit low points, the fears we had, the anger we felt, the resistance we each felt to changing, or even acknowledging that the other person might have a point. We talked about how pride got in our way at those times, and how useful we had found it to talk to one another, and to talk to someone else about the issues.

We can't say the evening was fun, but good friends need to be there for one another. Mostly we let them talk and tried not to give them advice, but to get them talking to each other. We encouraged them to seek couples counseling. The next day, Tammy told Dr. Hyman that they had stayed up half the night talking, and that it had opened a dialogue between them that felt helpful and hopeful.

8. Have I talked with my clergyperson?

Kenny, who is Jewish, was married to Olivia, who is Catholic. They didn't have any real problems with this until their first child got to be three years old and Olivia decided she wanted a Christmas tree. This had never come up before, but now it became a considerable source of conflict between them. Kenny put his foot down—no Christmas tree. Olivia put her foot down—I want one. They both dug their heels in, and whatever else was problematic in their marriage became expressed in this power struggle.

Kenny felt he would get support by going to talk to the rabbi at the synagogue he had gone to with his parents before he was married. The rabbi was an old man, and he was Orthodox, that is, very religious. He counseled Kenny, "You are married to a woman of another faith; you must respect that. You and she need to work together. Your children will be better for it. Your family is more important than a tree. Let her have the tree." Kenny

It usually takes a long time to get into marital troubles. It also takes a fair amount of time to get out of them.

was flabbergasted, but he went along with the wise guidance. It was the beginning of a thaw in their relationship.

Whether you actively practice your faith or not, consider seeking the counsel of a religious leader. You are likely to get a welcoming response, and, most often, thoughtful guidance.

9. Have we tried couples counseling? Have I tried individual counseling?

We want to remind you that people tend to wait too long to go into couples or individual counseling for it to be useful to their marriages. Additionally, a few sessions is not generally a cure-all. In fact, we know all too many people who have gone for a few sessions and then dropped out, only to say, "See, I tried and it didn't help." We recommend interviewing a counselor—or several—until you find someone you, or both of you, feel comfortable with, and who seems to understand your situation in a way that makes sense to you. You can locate counselors in your area through your family physician, your children's school psychologist, or using reputable Web sites, such as webmd.com or psychologytoday.com.

Julio went early enough, and has stayed in counseling long enough to make a real difference. Early in their marriage, Stella became fed up with Julio's use of drugs, which changed his personality so that he became insulting, bad-tempered, arrogant and disrespectful to her. He went into individual counseling. They are now married eight years and Julio has spoken extensively in counseling about these issues. In the counseling discussions, he also realized that he was treating colleagues disrespectfully at work, even though he is sober there. Julio has learned to keep his drug use and his unacceptable personality traits much more under control. Things are better between him and Stella; however, this has not been a magical solution. While they are still working on their marital problems, Julio thinks he might have been contemplating divorce by now if he hadn't learned to get better control of these problems in counseling.

10. Have we tried a trial separation as an almost last resort?

Virginia and Robert's marriage was entirely about Robert: his education, his career, his family, his religious beliefs, his everything. When Virginia found out that, despite her selfless devotion to all things "Robert," he was having a love affair with another woman, it was the last straw. She insisted that he move out, and they got a legal separation. But both of them postponed any conversation about divorcing.

They had joint custody of their two school-aged children, which left Virginia with some free time. She began to discover herself. She was able to convert her part-time job as a pharmaceutical representative, which she enjoyed, into a full-time job, and rapidly rose to a management position. She cultivated friends of her own and even started dating. For the first time, perhaps in her life, Virginia was getting feedback from the world about what an accomplished, talented, and attractive person she was.

Robert, for his part, was no longer the alpha male. He had to shop, cook, and clean for himself, and take care of his young children half of the week. The separation affected his rising star at his workplace, and suddenly he found that his career had stalled. Although she was single, he had no interest in marrying the woman he had had the affair with. Because of their shared parenting, he and Virginia continued to have extensive contact with each other. The more independent she became, the more attractive she was to Robert. The more he showed his vulnerable side, and the more he stepped up to properly parenting their children, the more attractive he became to her. It's rare that trial separations lead to marriages recovering. In this case, both Robert and Virginia went into individual counseling and worked a great deal on themselves. They have reconciled; they are back together. Lessons have been learned. They each have changed. The future is to be determined, but it looks much brighter.

Questions to Think About

1. Do I find aspects of my mate's behavior intolerable?
   Yes___No___

2. Have we grown apart? Yes___No___

3. Do we have too many different values? Yes___No___

4. Have I tried to improve myself? Have I gone along with my spouse's requests for change, but to no avail? Yes___No___

5. Have I fought for the relationship by negotiating, speaking up, and saying: "I am at the breaking point," but to no avail?
   Yes___No___

6. Have we tried spending more time, or less time together if that was useful, or needed, but to no avail? Yes___No___
7. Have I tried increasing our income, but to no avail? Yes___No___
8. Have I talked to clear-thinking friends, family, and/or clergy about my situation, but to no avail? Yes___No___
9. Have we tried couples and/or individual counseling, but to no avail? Yes___No___
10. Have we tried a trial separation, but to no avail? Yes___No___
11. Have I pretty much lost hope for change? Yes___No___
12. Do I believe I have exhausted every remedy? Yes___No___

Chapter 18

The Tipping Point

Marriages seldom end abruptly. Whether the couple realizes it or not, their relationship has been on a gradual downhill slide, which eventually brings the marriage to a tipping point. In this chapter we want you to hear people tell in their own words how they came to their decision. You want to know if it's time to go. Perhaps hearing the stories of other people's revelations of that moment will convince you that it's not time for you—or that it is. Their thoughts and conversations may sound familiar, but that doesn't mean your decision will be the same as theirs. We asked them to answer the following questions:

- What was the tipping point for them?
- When did they know their marriage must end?

Jack:

> I lost interest in her early on, but I stayed another thirty years. I took myself away mentally. The marriage wasn't good enough, but neither was it bad enough, so I stayed. We had children. We bought a house. I successfully pursued my career, but life was empty. I felt we were just going through the motions. Then one Saturday—I remember I had turned fifty-five the week before—we were at home, and someone came to the door for a charitable contribution. It was for a family who lived a couple of streets away whom we knew slightly. Their house had burned down. They had no insurance, and the husband, who was the breadwinner, had recently lost his job.
>
> My wife donated $5, which I thought was ridiculous. We were comfortable; we knew these people. It struck me that that was one of the things I disliked

about her so much. She was so uncharitable to people, including me. Right then I knew it was now or never. It finally had to be over between us.

Sharon:

I had a tough childhood. I grew up in a very troubled home. I had been rebelling against my parents since I was a teenager. My mother always stressed that anyone I dated should have "good breeding." My father wanted someone "manly" for me. After college, I got engaged to Dan. Dan's parents were both alcoholics, and they lived over a convenience store. When my best friend's mother met Dan, she said to me privately, "You know that he's gay, don't you?" I ignored her. I ignored my father and mother, too. At my wedding I got the shivers, and my dad said, "You know you don't have to go through with this."

Dan and I had never had sex or talked about it before we got married. I assumed it was because he was being refined and respectful. It never dawned on me that he had no experience with women. On our honeymoon, I knew I had made a terrible mistake. In his bathing suit he was so skinny and unmasculine—it was such a turnoff. I had to teach him everything about having sex.

I struggled for two years. We even had a child. One day we went to a drive-in movie with the baby. Sitting in the drive-in movie, I found it easier to say what was on my mind. I didn't have to look at Dan; I didn't have to see the shock or pain I was causing him. I just blurted out that I was miserable. I told him he had to move out.

Zach:

We got married outdoors by the sea on a beautiful June day. It was a perfect afternoon for a wedding. We had a big tent set up overlooking the water. All the guests were assembled. The minister was there. My wife-to-be looked beautiful, and I looked great, too. As the minister was making his introductory remarks about being gathered here, etc., from around a hundred yards away, out on the water, two young teenage boys, out in a little sailboat started yelling. They were far enough away so the sound was faint at first. Gradually, I became aware they were yelling at us. "Don't do it! Don't do it! Don't do it!" I tried to block it out of my mind, but, in hindsight, I'm sure everyone else also heard what they were yelling, but of course I ignored it and we married.

As time passed, the boys' taunts from my wedding day haunted me. My wife always had to be right. She was so stubborn and rigid. You could never get her to budge. She didn't understand anything about compromise. I wasn't aware of it bothering me that much in the beginning, but the longer we were married, the more I found those qualities drove me crazy and pushed me away. There was no softness from her. It was the major thing I talked about in the counseling we went to. After two years, the marriage counselor said to us that I was trying harder than my wife was to make the marriage work, and my wife admitted it. She didn't think she needed to change, no matter how unhappy I was. She said, "That's who I am!" At that moment I finally believed her.

I had never really gotten the image of those boys on my wedding day out of my mind. I'm sure, somehow, I knew at the time they were right. It just took me ten years to admit it to myself.

Rita:

Arnie and I had been living together for two years when we got married. He got really drunk at our wedding. My best friend was sitting on his lap, and he was hitting on her. He had my sister in tears telling her how fat she looked in her bridesmaid's dress. I cried all the way to our honeymoon.

Three years into our marriage I developed breast cancer and had to have a mastectomy. That's when his flirtations with other women started getting really serious. One night we were having dinner at some friends' house. There was a pretty woman, another man's date, sitting next to my husband. All through the night their chairs kept turning more and more toward each other. Arnie talked to her nonstop. Then I saw them exchange cards. Not too long after that he started coming home late and drunk, and telling me he had to stay late with clients. I found motel receipts in his pockets sometimes. Once he came home at 6 a.m. and told me he had fallen asleep drunk in the car.

I knew he was cheating, but I couldn't bring myself to confront him. I was a Stepford wife. I was so dependent on him. I didn't work. I had been his "sex kitten." From the time of the mastectomy, he rejected me. Instead of coming to bed, he'd stay up late watching pornography by himself. It was so painful to me. He told me that I was lucky that I had him and that no one else would want me—that I was damaged goods. I had reconstructive surgery, but I still had totally lost confidence in myself.

Then I met Ben in a cooking class at the local community college. I started having an affair with him. He told me that I was really beautiful; he accepted me as I was. One night, when Arnie was away for the weekend on a motorcycle trip, I invited Ben to the house for dinner. I planned a romantic night. I met him at the door in a filmy negligee.

Ben and I were in the middle of dinner when I heard Arnie's key unexpectedly opening the door. He was a day early coming home. It was like a scene from the movie *Five Easy Pieces*. Arnie grabbed the tablecloth and yanked it. The dishes and food all went flying. That was the moment I knew it was over. Ben left. Arnie went berserk. He said, "Get out." I said, "No, you get out." He hit me, but he left the next day.

José:

I was raised Catholic. My marriage wasn't horrible, but it was deadening. I was trained to be self-effacing, to do what needed to be done, not to do what I felt. We were very different people, but we had two girls. I worked for the governor's office and when he went to Washington, D.C. to Congress, he recruited me to go with him. That was the moment I knew there was a way out. I never said, "I'm not coming back," but I knew it.

Melanie:

I went to live with him in Canada, where he was from. At that time, the law there was that a woman was literally chattel. He owned everything we had, including my body. I had no legal rights in our home—zip. He acted toward me as if he owned me. Something would set him off and he'd go nuts; I was really frightened. I must have known I was going to go when I hid the spare car keys in the car in case I had to make an escape.

It was a winter night. We were getting ready for bed. I was naked. He started having a meltdown and accused me of wanting to leave him. He made a big gesture of grabbing his car keys that were on the table. I ran out onto the driveway naked and he slammed the door on me, in the middle of winter in Canada. I got in the car, just like that, and drove away. I never saw him again, but a couple of years later the police contacted me. He had committed suicide.

Jennifer:

I knew things were wrong from the beginning. I had so many doubts about marrying Liam that I took a survey of my friends. Marrying him won, but only by a small margin.

Liam was successful, charming, good-looking, and his alcoholism, he reassured me, had been under control for several years. It was true—he didn't drink at all. Still, I had always been a little troubled by his mood swings. Some days he'd come home and he'd be "the life of the party," full of jokes and conversation. Some days he'd be withdrawn and solitary. But I put it out of my mind and married him.

When we were married for about nine months, I was in the bathroom one day, and happened to look up at the ceiling. The light fixture looked like it had accumulated a lot of dust and dirt in it. I got a stepladder, and climbed up to take the glass cover down to clean it. Liam had a veritable drugstore of pills hidden there—uppers, downers, who knows? I was heartsick. The only person I could think of to call was my mother-in-law. When I told her about the pills, and asked her what I should do, she said: "That's your problem, honey," and hung up on me. Thinking about that and other things later, I came to understand that my mother-in-law was an addict, too. I packed and left immediately with no forwarding address.

Donna:

We always had a lot of friends over to our house. So when Ed's fiftieth birthday was coming, I knew everyone would expect me to make something special for him. I invited our whole crowd, and some of the family, probably thirty people in all. I asked a number of people to prepare a toast to Ed in advance. The toast idea was a big mistake. For weeks before the party I drove myself crazy trying to think of what to say, even though I am good at that sort of thing. I couldn't come up with anything that would be honest. I talked to my best friend about it. She said, "You have to make a toast."

I no longer admired my husband. I no longer loved him. I didn't think he was a great father, or a great husband, or a great friend. It just hit me like a ton of bricks, because of the need to write the toast. It wasn't that I was unaware of how I felt, it was that I had reached the end of the line. I couldn't tell a flat-out lie in front of everyone I did love and care about.

So the night of the party, a lot of people made toasts. When it came to my turn, I just raised my glass and weakly said: "To Ed." That's all. A strange thing happened to me. As the last guests were leaving, I started to cry. I couldn't stop. I had had a couple of drinks, but, more importantly, the house started feeling so empty. I was going to be left with Ed, which somehow seemed lonelier than being alone. Ed moved out six months later.

Hank:

My marriage of eighteen years had not been going well for a long time. Sheila and I had tried everything. We had made promises to each other, which we promptly broke. We had joined a marriage group in our church. We stayed a couple of months and then decided it wasn't working. We were just living our lives very separately from one another, with our two teenage sons, but with no joy.

A woman I had met in the pastoral counseling group and I had become friends. About a year later, when nothing at all had improved in my marriage, I'm a little embarrassed to say, she and I became lovers. She and her husband had separated. After we had been together for a few months, she went to visit a girlfriend in California. The day after she left, I impulsively told my wife that I was going to leave our marriage. She didn't have a big reaction. She asked me why, but she didn't protest, either. This was in December, and we calmly decided that I would move out at the end of the school year in June.

The next day I did something I had never done before. I e-mailed my sweetheart a romantic love note. Twenty-four hours later I was at work and I got a call from my wife confessing that she had been looking at my outgoing e-mail and had discovered my love note. My wife demanded that I come home immediately. I couldn't, I was in the middle of an important meeting, but I said I'd be home in a few hours.

Even though I had already announced that I was leaving, I was furious with myself. I should never have sent the e-mail.

It was a nightmare, but then I realized that maybe this wasn't so terrible after all. I was starting to feel a huge sense of relief. I don't know if I would have had the courage to move out at the end of June, as I had said I was going to. This forced me to decide.

Sheila, who had been so matter-of-fact two days earlier when I had told her I was going to move out, suddenly was now completely hysterical, saying, "Let's try again, but you must give up this other woman." When I said I would not try again, it's too late, she told me I had to move out by the end of the month.

Kathryn:

It was Valentine's Day. Even though I felt my husband hadn't been my Valentine for years, I felt obliged to buy him a card. I had waited until the last minute. We had never stopped being polite to each other, and going through the motions, but our relationship could hardly be called a marriage, more a financial arrangement. I spent a long time in the card store; every card seemed wrong because it expressed feelings I didn't have and didn't want to convey. Finally, I found a card that I thought was okay. It was a childish cartoon: It wasn't loving; it wasn't nasty; it was silly and rhyming and really didn't say anything at all. It expressed my feelings of emptiness perfectly.

That night we exchanged cards. When I opened the one he gave me, it was a knife in my heart. He had picked out the exact same card for me that I bought him. I knew it wasn't a coincidence. I also knew our marriage was over.

Wes:

I was really blind to what was going on for the last few years of my marriage. I now see I just couldn't face reality. My best friend, Art, had become more and more a part of our lives. We—my wife, Art, and I—did everything together. He spent more time at our house than at his. I really enjoyed having him around. I thought we were all having a great time. Art's a lot of fun. He's a great cook. He always has good ideas about things to do, the right movie, a good new restaurant. Art never had a woman around. In the back of my mind I thought he might be gay, although it was something we never spoke about. Janet liked him as much as I did, in hindsight, more.

I don't know how I could have missed all the signals. I'd come home from work and Art and Janet would be making dinner for the three of us. If Janet needed to go somewhere, Art would volunteer to drive her. I was completely blown away when Janet said to me that she and Art were going to go on a vacation together, without me. I said, "You can't do that. If you go away with Art on a vacation, don't ever come back." She said, "We're going." Suddenly, the lights came on. I understood what had happened. It was over. They are married to each other now.

Courtney:

My husband and I were in the LA Airport. It was really crowded, as only the LA Airport can be. We were on what felt like an endless line to get to the ticket counter. I wasn't really looking forward to this trip. All Larry ever wanted to do on a vacation was lie around a pool, broil in the sun, and read. What's the point of being in Mexico, or anywhere else, if you are going to do the same thing you do all the time at home?

Don't get me wrong—Larry is a decent guy. In fact, that is part of his problem. Life was really boring with him. Everyone took advantage of him. Even at restaurants the bills were always wrong, never in our favor. It's as if people spotted him a mile away. If we had work done in the yard, or on the house, the workmen overcharged us, and Larry never said a word.

Anyway, we were on that line in the airport, and people, one after another, probably about a half a dozen of them, kept cutting in front of us. Letting that happen seemed to me to express Larry's whole point of view in life: "Don't make waves." In that moment in the airport I knew I just couldn't continue like this.

Phillip:

I didn't realize that my wife's mental health had been deteriorating for years. She was accusing me of cheating on her and having sex with numerous other women. I was always faithful to her, but she was so convinced, that at one point I started doubting my own sanity, and briefly thought that maybe I was! She even accused me of having sex with our neighbors, both the husband and the wife. She'd come into our living room and say she smelled sex in the room.

We were married thirty years and we had a twenty-eight-year-old son. When we had good times, we were ecstatic. The bad times were a nightmare. First it was 70/30 good and bad, then 60/40, 50/50, then 40/60; the bad just got worse and worse. We had been going downhill for maybe ten years. I knew I was unhappy, but I didn't see any way out.

She'd watch the Home Shopping Network and order all kinds of things. We'd have battles about money all the time. I was running as fast as I could to pay off the credit cards. I didn't see how I could leave her and manage financially. She had never worked. The last three years we were barely talking. She had moved into our son's old room.

One night we were having an argument about money, and the next thing I knew a squad car pulled up to the house. When I answered the door, they said she had called in a complaint that I had assaulted her. Actually, she had tried to hit me and I had pushed her away. The cops came in. One talked to me, the other talked to her in another room. Eventually they cuffed me and took me to jail. I called my mother. She couldn't believe where I was. She came down and bailed me out. A couple of days later the charges were dropped.

I went to live at my mother's house. This gave me stability and a base for four months. I never thought I'd be able to manage two households financially, but you find out that you can. After living with my mother, I got my own place. Why did I stay in my marriage so long? She tore me down all the time and I guess I eventually believed her; I thought I deserved it. In retrospect, I understand it's like the Stockholm syndrome. You begin to believe what you are told. I've grown from it. I've picked myself up.

Albert:

I had to go on a lengthy business trip to China. It would last at least a month. I had wanted her to take our little girl and come on the trip with me, but she didn't want to go. When I got off the plane, I knew from her icy greeting that it was over. She greeted me like a stranger. Part of me hoped that it was another one of her depressive episodes. There had been several before. Once she had attempted suicide, slit her wrists, and was hospitalized for more than a month. That time I also was just arriving back from a business trip. A policeman met me when I got off the plane. He told me my wife was in the hospital and that he would take me there.

I used to feel, "What had I done? What had set her off into such an awful place?" I would go over and over it in my mind, replaying every word I could think of, every interchange that had taken place between us, but I could never find a cause and effect, at least not one to set her off so badly.

After she was diagnosed as manic-depressive, I began to feel a little less to blame, although I still couldn't help questioning myself. We were both young and inexperienced when we got married. I think I was only her second boyfriend. She was my second girlfriend. In retrospect, I think she married me just to have a baby. She didn't want a husband. Her mother hadn't wanted a husband, either.

> This time it was like—I've seen this before, but she really seemed to mean it when she said she wanted a divorce. I was devastated at first—I really loved her. Still, sooner than I expected, I began to feel better.

Sophie:

> I married one day after my eighteenth birthday. My mother had died the previous year and my father remarried. I was an impediment to them. I married a very nice guy. I knew in the back of my mind it wouldn't last forever when I married him. He was good to me. He helped me get through college, and I got a good job. We had two children. The day I turned thirty it hit me like a ton of bricks. All I could think of was "Is this all there is?" I had been bored out of my mind in this marriage for five years. There was no one else in my life, but I got it into my head that I had to see what it would be like on my own. I felt that my kids and I would be okay, and that eventually I'd meet someone else.

We can't predict what your tipping point might be or tell you definitely when you need to go. You need to decide for yourself. But by relying on the tools we have given you in this book, you should have a better idea. You will know if you have done what you can or are willing to do to fight for your relationship, but nonetheless expect to have mixed feelings no matter what you decide.

CHAPTER 19

Making Your Plan

Step 10: Decide—What's my plan?

Most people make a break in a moment of intense emotion with no plan in place. In fact, many people don't even acknowledge that they are at the breaking point until they snap. If you have decided it is time to go, we encourage you to be thoughtful and deliberate for the sake of everyone in the family. If you separate precipitously, you may cause an extra degree of hurt to your children or your spouse or leave yourself vulnerable to being taken advantage of by your spouse in his or her hurt and angry reaction to your leaving. It's better to have a plan. A good plan is to adopt a set of goals for you and your children's well-being. We suggest these five goals for your plan.

- Minimize conflict
- Protect your financial interests
- Watch out for your children's well-being
- Develop a support system
- Be decisive; get it over with

Minimize Conflict

If you and your partner were in a high-conflict marriage, the conflict is likely to continue into your separation and divorce. In the course of a separation, some couples are drawn into fighting with one another even more frequently and angrily than they did during the worst times of their marriage. Our goal of minimizing conflict applies specifically to those couples. If this is you, get a lawyer right away, and communicate with your ex as much as possible through your attorney. The attorney doesn't have to be belligerent or try to take advantage of your ex, as this would be unfair and provoke more conflict. The attorney needs to guide you through a settlement the two of you can live with. The purpose of this is to reduce conflict to the lowest level feasible because conflict is so damaging to everyone, but especially your children. Let your two attorneys talk to each other and convey your wishes.

If you were in a low-conflict relationship, mediation may be a much better and less expensive choice, but you both have to be willing to compromise on almost every issue.

It's hard to resist the temptation to fight back with a belligerent, provocative ex, but if you stop to think about it, conflict is really a way of continuing the intense relationship between you and your partner, a way of staying connected. If you've made the decision to terminate the relationship, endless fighting only keeps it going. This is easier said than done, especially when your ex provokes you with punitive, unreasonable, and what you might consider irresponsible demands. So limit your contact with your ex-spouse as much as possible. Don't hang around. Don't go into the house or invite him in during visitation exchanges. Limit telephone conversations to logistics surrounding the children or moving furniture. Make yourself scarce. Try not to take the bait if your ex provokes you. You have nothing to gain by alienating him further. You will never convince him that you were right and he was wrong, and vice versa. That's why you're divorcing. Realize that the reason you have decided to go is because you two cannot agree on most things. Fighting with one another now is just more of the same. You can't control your spouse's behavior. Let it go.

Protect Your Financial Interests

Before you announce that you are going to leave, make sure you know what your marital assets are, and where they are, including knowing all your bank accounts, stock portfolios, IRAs, safe deposit boxes and keys, insurance policies, tax records, and contact information for accountants, bankers, and insurance agents. If you have time and access, set some money aside. Figure out where your income will be coming from after you separate and divorce. Will it be from alimony and child support, from work, from savings, from sales of assets, from family? You need to know.

Is there something you and your spouse own that you can't live without? Do you feel you must stay in the house? Do you feel you could never part with your dad's coin collection? If there is something really important to you of material value, think about that now, and speak about what you value and what you don't to the mediator or your attorney.

Protect Your Children

You have been thinking about leaving for a long time. That puts you toward the end of a long process. Your children probably don't know anything about this, even as you are reading this book. When you and your spouse tell your children that you are separating—and we hope you do that together—it will just be the beginning for them. You are ready to accept this change. They will likely rebel against it for some time to come. Be patient and sympathetic toward them until they get used to it. Be positive about the future all of you will have.

Calm their anxieties. If they won't live with you, show them where you plan to live. Hopefully, it will be nearby. Confirm to them that they will be able to stay in their same house, school, and keep their same friends as much as possible (assuming that's the case). If you have a relatively amicable relationship with your ex, you may be able to co-parent your children, that is, act jointly in their best interests. No matter how you feel about your ex, support visitation. If you have a high-conflict relationship with your ex, you will need to let her parent in her own way without you trying to control her, even though you may want to, unless you are absolutely convinced that your child's safety is at risk with her. Then you should try to talk calmly to her, but, if that fails, have your attorney write a letter about your concerns to her. In other words, continue to try to minimize conflict between the two of you, but do not ignore danger to avoid possible conflict.

Your children need two parents. Accept that exchanges of the children are likely to be rocky for a while for everyone. Try to enjoy the time when you don't have your children with you. Spend some of it taking care of yourself, so you can be supportive of their needs when you are with them.

Develop a Support System

Adults in the 160-family study done by psychologist Abigail Stewart in Boston pointed out that having someone to talk to who had gone through or was going through a divorce was a great solace for them. You may already have a sister, brother, neighbor, friend, or coworker who is a good listener, and has enough of the same experience you are having to be a sympathetic one. If you don't, seek one out. Consider joining a divorce support group. Many are free of charge and run by local religious, social service groups, or hospitals.Remember that, as we mentioned earlier, nine out of ten separations and divorces are amicable.

There is always emotional and practical value in getting a chance to air your concerns, finding out that they are legitimate, and hearing how others are dealing with similar situations creatively and effectively.

Be kind to yourself. Stay away from negative people and limit contact or discussions of your situation with friends or family who are not supportive. Years of living in a bad marriage is very debilitating to a person's self-confidence, and self-image. You may need to work on strengthening your self-esteem. A good place to do that, and to get advice on how to deal most effectively with your children and your ex-spouse, is through therapy or counseling. If your finances are strapped, and you don't have insurance, you may be able to identify a mental health clinic in your area where they have sliding-scale fees based on income.

Be Decisive; Get It Over With

The decision to separate and to end your marriage, deciding it is time to go, is a decision that will shape your life, your spouse's, and, to a lesser extent, your children's lives, for the rest of all of your lives. Few decisions we can think of rival divorce in its impact. We've spoken to hundreds of people about their marriages and their divorces. Some look back, having lost someone they loved, and regret that they were immature, stubborn, and resistant to change that might have saved their marriage. But the reality is that at the time they did not make those changes in the relationship they were in, and perhaps, because of the loss they endured, they developed greater self-awareness and maturity. Almost no one who initiated a divorce said they regretted it. On the contrary, almost everyone who initiated a divorce regretted waiting so long.

Most people are moved by the following section of the New Testament, I Corinthians 13 (New International Version), and we add our voices to the chorus: ". . . but [if I] have not love, I am nothing. . . . And now these three remain: faith, hope, and love, but the greatest of these is love." The love in Corinthians can be any kind of love—marital love; romantic love; the love of children, family, and friends; of your work and your commitments; the love of the God you worship. Corinthians tells us we should surround ourselves with love. Perhaps it is time to go if your marriage does not provide you with that love, and encourage your capacity to love. For without love, there is nothing.

APPENDICES

The Marriage Test

The Marriage Test is a compilation of all the questions of all the chapters in *How to Know If It's Time to Go*. This is not a scientific test. Take it and see how your marriage rates. A score of more than 50 percent "yes" may mean you are facing real risk in your marriage. Of course, you have to make your own decision, and we highly recommend that you seek professional help before taking any drastic steps.

1. Do my spouse and I disagree on at least three of the nine areas (see page 3) in which all couples must work out agreements? Yes___No___
2. Have our persistent disagreements led to open or hidden anger and disrespect between us? Yes___No___
3. For the most part, have my spouse and I stopped trying to please each other in the areas that really matter to each of us? Yes___No___
4. Do I feel the scorecard of "rights and wrongs" between us is strongly out of balance? Yes___No___
5. Is there too great an imbalance of power between us in the relationship? Yes___No___
6. Are we stuck in habits we formed when we were much less mature people? Yes___No___
7. Do we avoid spending time together? Yes___No___

8. Do I feel more respected and accepted by a family member, a same-sex friend, or a colleague than I do by my spouse? Yes___No___
9. Do I feel my mate is not sufficiently loyal to me? Yes___No___
10. Do I feel my mate is not sufficiently protective of me? Yes___No___
11. Do I feel my marriage lacks affection? Yes___No___
12. Is there an unfair division of labor in my marriage? Yes___No___
13. Has my mate let me down when I needed physical or emotional caring? Yes___No__
14. Do I feel taken for granted in my marriage? Yes___No___
15. Do I lack sufficient companionship in my marriage? Yes___No___
16. Do my spouse and I compete for our children's loyalty and affection? Yes___No___
17. Is one or the other of us substituting closeness with our children for marital intimacy? Yes___No___
18. Has our home stopped being the place where we each feel emotionally safe and accepted? Yes___No___
19. Have one or both of us dropped out of the family, clearly preferring outside career and social interests to family life? Yes___No___
20. Do we play "good cop/bad cop" with our children's discipline because one of us sees the other as too harsh or too lenient? Yes___No___
21. Do I shudder when qualities I don't like in my mate surface in our children? Yes___No___
22. Can I think of any recent incidents in which one of our children has called attention to himself by getting into trouble, or in some other negative way? Yes___No___

23. Do I blame our child's repeated misbehavior, in or out of school, on the child, or my spouse, or on myself, and never look at these problems as a symptom of the struggles in our marriage? Yes___No___

24. Do I feel it is possible that the conflict in our marriage could indirectly be causing misbehavior or lowered school performance in our children? Yes___No___

25. Am I becoming convinced that two full-time parents who agree on little are not as wholesome an environment for children as a stable, low-conflict, single-parent home? Yes___No___

26. As a barometer of our marriage, is our sex life indicating that the climate is too cool? Yes___No___

27. Does one of us say no to a sexual overture from the other more than 25 percent of the time? Yes___No___

28. Are we unable to talk about our sex life? Yes___No___

29. Do our weekends revolve almost entirely around household responsibilities, taking our children to activities, and socializing with other adults, with little or no time spent just with each other? Yes___No___

30. Are one or both of us susceptible to the attractiveness of others because we no longer feel we are with our best possible partner? Yes___No___

31. Does one of us have an opposite-sex friend who provides either sexual or nonsexual intimacy that we don't have in our marriage? Yes___No___

32. Are most of the couples we socialize with unhappily married or divorced? Yes___No___

33. Is it possible that the lack of energy, sleep problems, irritability, lack of enthusiasm, or depression I experience is a result of our unhappy marriage? Yes___No___

34. Does anyone in our family overeat compulsively, suffer from obesity, anorexia or bulimia, or use alcohol, drugs, or mood-altering medications excessively? Yes___No___

35. Do the interactions between us make me feel less attractive and less cherished, rather than bolstering my good feelings about myself? Yes___No___

36. Do I feel I can do little right in my spouse's opinion, or she in mine? Yes___No___

37. Might the negative interactions between us be hurting our children's self-confidence and self-esteem? Yes___No___

38. Has either of us had any serious accidents that might be attributable to the distraction and depression that comes from our poor relationship? Yes___No___

39. Does anyone in our family suffer from physical problems that are linked to stress? (See pages 56 and 57.) Is it possible that marital discord is contributing to making one of us sick? Yes___No___

40. Is it possible that I have been waiting too long for this "rough patch" in my marriage to end? Yes___No___

41. Do I stay, in part, because I am afraid no one else will want me? Yes___No___

42. Do I stay, in part, because I am ashamed to admit to myself, my friends, or my family, that my marriage isn't working? Yes___No___

43. Do I stay, in part, because I am afraid that I will just make the same mistakes again if I divorce and eventually remarry? Yes___ No___

44. Do I stay, in part, because I am afraid that if I divorce I will be financially ruined? Yes___No___

45. If we separate, can I accept it if my mate finds someone else who makes him happier than I have? Yes___No___

46. Do I stay, in part, because I am afraid my mate will reject or neglect our children if we divorce? Yes___No___

47. Is one or both of us frequently trying to demonstrate the other's shortcomings, mistakes, or inadequacies? Yes___No___

48. Does one or both of us usually try to gain the upper hand to prove the other wrong and blame him in a crisis, rather than seeing the crisis as happening to "us"? Yes___No___

49. When I think about separating, am I unable to take a long-term view, but focus primarily on the disruption I'll face short term? Yes___No___

50. Am I aware of the cumulative effects that our unhappy marriage is having on me and the rest of our family, and that the longer I stay, the more we all feel them? Yes___No___

51. Do my spouse and I communicate using the win/lose model? Yes___No___

52. Are our children frequently exposed to ongoing conflict between my spouse and me? Yes___No___

53. Am I afraid to separate, in part, because I fear our children's anger and possible rejection? Yes___No___

54. Am I afraid that if I am the noncustodial parent I will lose touch with my children's daily lives? Yes___No___

55. Are our children growing up in an unhappy intact family? Yes___No___

56. Do we often argue about our children? Yes___No___

57. Are we often incapable of pulling together to act jointly to help our child address behavior and school performance issues? Yes___No___

58. Are my spouse and I engaged in a power struggle? Yes___No___

59. Do I worry about the quality of my relationship with my son or daughter? Yes___No___

60. Do I worry about the quality of my spouse's relationship with our son or daughter? Yes___No___

61. Am I afraid that our children will be burdened with worry if I divorce? Yes___No___

62. Do I stay in my marriage, in part, because I don't feel I am capable of making all the decisions that I would have to make solo if I divorced? Yes___No___

63. Am I aware of changes that my spouse has repeatedly wanted me to make and I have been unable or unwilling to make? Yes___No___

64. Am I aware of changes I have repeatedly wanted my spouse to make that he has been unable or unwilling to make? Yes___No___

65. Could it be that stubbornness, defensiveness, and resistance to criticism are preventing both of us from changing? Yes___No___

66. Do I think that my spouse dismisses some of my concerns because she doesn't believe I would ever leave our marriage? Yes___No___

67. Have we avoided the "crucible" of completely open and honest conversation about our problems? Yes___No___

68. Do I feel I have outgrown my mate? Yes___No___

69. Do I feel my self-confidence has been hurt by the disregard and disrespect in my marriage? Yes___No___

70. Do I feel my maturation, growth, and development as a person, as a professional, or as a parent have been hindered by my marriage? Yes___No___

71. Am I young enough to feel I can make a new beginning, finish or extend my education, build or start my career? Or, am I old enough so that I have built a career and saved some money so I have a safety net? Yes___ No___

72. Am I prepared to make some financial sacrifices if I need to? Yes___No___

73. Can I tolerate a dispute over money, if my spouse forces one? Yes___No___

74. Are there enough assets so that each of us will be able to go forward and manage? Yes___No___

75. Can I generate some alternative child care if I need to work? Yes___No___

76. Is there anyone else whom I could share expenses with or get help from if I divorce? Yes___No___

77. Could I increase my energy and commitment to my career or work so I could potentially increase my earnings? Yes___No___

78. Am I using fear of financial hardship as an excuse for staying in my marriage because of other fears that are harder to think about? Yes___No___

79. Has my marriage suffered because of a significant change in my family's finances, either down or up? Yes___No___

80. Am I prepared to give up this person I once loved? Yes___ No___

81. Am I prepared to share custody of my children and not see them every day? Yes___No___

82. Am I prepared to give up some of the current structure of my life, and some of my normal routines, and even some of my friends and relatives? Yes___No___

83. Am I prepared for my husband/wife to give me a difficult time when it comes to child rearing and/or visitation? Yes___No___

84. Am I prepared to possibly face bitterness or retaliation from my ex if I divorce? Yes___No___

85. Can I handle life in a "couples' world" and build a network of support without my mate? Yes___No___

86. Can I get past feelings of failure or shame if I divorce? Yes___No___

87. Am I prepared for my children's behavior to get more difficult while they are getting used to a changed family structure? Yes___No___

88. Am I prepared not to raise my children in the same household with their mother/father? Yes___No___

89. Do I find aspects of my mate's behavior intolerable? Yes___No___

90. Have we grown apart? Yes___No___

91. Do we have too many different values? Yes___No___

92. Have I tried to improve myself? Have I gone along with my spouse's requests for change, but to no avail? Yes___No___

93. Have I fought for the relationship by negotiating, speaking up, and saying, "I am at the breaking point," but to no avail? Yes___No___

94. Have we tried spending more time, or less time, together if that was useful, or needed, but to no avail? Yes___No___

95. Have I tried increasing our income, but to no avail? Yes___No___

96. Have I talked to clear-thinking friends, family, and/or clergy about my situation, but to no avail? Yes___No___

97. Have we tried couples and/or individual counseling, but to no avail? Yes___No___

98. Have we tried a trial separation, but to no avail? Yes___No___

99. Have I pretty much lost hope for change? Yes___No___

100. Do I believe I have exhausted every remedy? Yes___No___

My score: Yes_______No_______

Selected Annotated Bibliography

The literature about divorce is vast, confusing, and often contradictory, and each year adds several important and thoughtful additions. What follows is a selection of notable works that pertain to the specific discussions in our chapters. We have not listed reference works for chapters 16–19, as they, more than the other chapters, derive solely from our own original research.

Introduction

Furstenberg, Frank, and Andrew Cherlin. (1994). *Divided Families: What Happens to Children When Parents Part.* Cambridge, Mass.: Harvard University Press.

These researchers studied the data collected in the 1981 National Survey of Children, which included over fifteen thousand children. They compared relationships, school achievements, and behavior of children from divorced families with children from intact families. They also compared the quality of the relationships of children with their custodial parent versus their noncustodial parent. They found that children's behavior and schoolwork remained the same or improved by two years after their parents had separated when they were compared with their behavior and school performance prior to separation. They also found that, too often, the relationship between the noncustodial parents and their children deteriorated over time, especially if the parents continued a high level of conflict after the divorce.

Wallerstein, Judith, and Sandra Blakeslee. (1990). *Second Chances.* New York: Ticknor & Fields.

———. (2000). *The Unexpected Legacy of Divorce: A Twenty-Five Year Landmark Study.* New York: Hyperion.

In her own clinic, Judith Wallerstein studies sixty white, middle-class, divorced California families, including 131 children. This is a longitudinal study that began in 1971. Wallerstein's hypothesis is that divorce injures children in a variety of ways. Still, she acknowledges much resilience in children and adolescents as they recover within a few years after their parents' divorce. She states that women, in particular, feel better off emotionally and usually have recovered financially several years after their divorce.

Chapter 1

Gottman, John. (1993). *Why Marriages Succeed or Fail.* New York: Simon and Schuster.

One aspect of Gottman's work with couples at the University of Washington is to assess the impact on their marriages of the way in which they argue. He finds that when happily married couples argue, most of the time they stick to the subject, practice restraint, resort to humor, and show some flexibility. Happily married couples usually have about five positive interactions for every one negative interaction. Gottman finds that when unhappy couples argue, they resort to harsh criticism of one another, defensiveness, contempt, and stubbornness.

Peterson, James, and Nicholas Zill. (1983). "The Life Course of Children of Divorce: Marital Disruption and Parental Conflict," *American Sociological Review* 48 (5): 656–668.

———. (1986). "Marital Disruption, Parent-Child Relationships and Behavior Problems in Children," *Journal of Marriage and the Family* 48: 295–307.

At the time of these publications, Peterson and Zill were directors of the Children of Divorce Project at the National Institute of Health. Their studies include data on more than fourteen hundred families, both divorced and intact, with children aged twelve to sixteen. One question they sought to answer in their research was this: "What creates marital conflict?" Through their investigations, they found the nine areas that couples invariably must come to resolution about.

Chapter 4

Hetherington, E. Mavis, and John Kelly. (2002). *For Better or for Worse: Divorce Reconsidered.* New York: W. W. Norton and Company.

Professor Hetherington is emeritus in the Department of Psychology at the University of Virginia. Her life work has been devoted to the impact of unhappy marriages and divorce on children. This book reports on the whole body of her work, which has taken place over thirty years and included more than twenty five hundred children and fourteen hundred families. The families she studied included those who were separated, divorced, or remarried. Hetherington's research leads her to conclude that conflict between parents is the single most stressful experience for children, whether the conflict is during the marriage or after it. She finds that when divorces settle down children and adults are remarkably resilient.

Rutter, Michael. (1985). "Resilience in the Face of Adversity: Protective Factors and Resistance to Psychiatric Disorder," *British Journal of Psychiatry* 147: 598–611.

Sir Michael Rutter is a professor of psychiatry at Kings College, University of London. He has written widely on delinquency behavior among teenage boys from all social and economic groups. He is particularly interested in what motivates criminal and delinquent behavior. In this study, he found that boys from high-conflict intact families shoplifted more often and had a higher incidence of other delinquent behaviors than teenage boys from low-conflict divorced families. This was found to be true irrespective of the boys' economic and social class.

Stewart, Abigail, J., *et al.* (1997). *Separating Together: How Divorce Transforms Families.* New York: The Guilford Press.

Abigail Stewart and her colleagues conducted their study in the Greater Boston area with one hundred and sixty divorcing families with school-aged children between the ages of six and twelve. The study included both mothers and fathers, mostly the custodial parents. It looked at people from different income levels, ethnicity, educational backgrounds, religions who had divorced or separated for a variety of reasons. The study is extremely comprehensive. Stewart interviewed all participants at various stages after their separations. In addition, she looked at a wide range of variables. She compares divorcing families with a non-divorced control group. Stewarts' findings put to rest many common negative misperceptions about divorcing and divorced families.

Chapter 6

Dube, Shanta, and DeLisa Fairweather, *et al.* (2009). "Cumulative Childhood Stress and Auto-immune Diseases in Adults," *Psychosomatic Medicine* 71:243–250.

Gottman, John. (1993). *Why Marriages Succeed or Fail.* New York: Simon and Schuster.

Kiecolt-Glaser, Janice. (2001). "Marriage, Health and Immune Function in Relational Processes in Mental Health." Arlington, Virginia: American Psychiatric Publications.

Marcenas, W. S., *et al.* (1993). "The Relationship Between Self Reported Symptoms and Life Events," *Journal of Psychology and Health* 8: 123–134.

The articles and books listed above all discuss research results from studies done with adults and children from unhappy families and marriages, both divorced and intact. Each study demonstrates the highly significant correlation between unhappy family and marital life and a wide range of medical illnesses.

Chapter 7

Amato, Paul R., and B. Keith. (1991). "Parental divorce and the well-being of children," *Psychological Bulletin* 110: 26–46.

Paul Amato is a lifelong researcher on the influence of divorce on families and children. Amato's findings in this study suggest that as divorce has become more frequent and, at the same time more acceptable, there are fewer negative effects on children's school performance and behavior. Amato studied children whose parents divorced during three different periods of time: 1950–1969, 1970–1979, and 1980–1989. With each succeeding time period, as divorce has grown more common and less stigmatizing in American society, the overall severity of divorce's impact has decreased for the children who are involved in it.

Braver, Sanford, and Diane O'Connell. (1999). *Divorced Dads: Shattering the Myths.* New York: Tarcher/Putnam.

In research funded by the National Institute of Mental Health, Braver and O'Connell found that most widely held notions about divorced fathers are untrue. For example, the vast majority of divorced fathers do not abandon their families, do pay child support, do not impoverish their former wives and children, and, as long as they stay involved with their children, personally benefit both psychologically and financially from their continued involvement. These are the researchers who laid to rest Lenore Weitzman's widely influential claims about how women suffer financially after divorce.

Coontz, Stephanie. (1997). *The Way We Really Are: Coming to Terms with America's Changing Families.* New York: Basic.

Coontz explores traditions in the American family, including those surrounding divorce. She helps readers understand the stresses and strains on their family lives that lead to conflict and disruption. She helps us recognize how over-attachment to traditional ideas can lead us to false expectations, judgments, and bias of what marriage and family life are supposed to be like. She also reflects on the impact of false expectations about parenting and children's growth and development.

Nofsinger, Mary M. (1990). *Children and Adjustment to Divorce: An Annotated Bibliography.* New York: Garland.

After comprehensively compiling more than six hundred different references on children's adjustment to divorce, Nofsinger concludes that divorce research is both confusing and contradictory. Still, she states that more and more studies lend support to the view that divorce can be beneficial in the long run as an alternative to an unhappy family situation. There are serious short-term psychological stressors that many children experience as a result of their parents' unhappy marriage and its break-up, but these last for a limited period of time, subsiding after a few transitional years.

Chapter 9

Stewart, Abigail, J., *et al.* (1997). *Separating Together: How Divorce Transforms Families.* New York: The Guilford Press.

In addition to work previously described, Stewart points out that after a transition period of a few years following separation, things settle down. She states that it's important to recognize that benefits will not be fully evident until the transition period is over. She describes that this period lasts from one to three years following separation.

Chapter 10

Furstenberg, Frank, and Andrew Cherlin. (1994). *Divided Families: What Happens to Children When Parents Part.* Cambridge, Mass: Harvard University Press.

Hetherington, E. Mavis, and John Kelly. (2002). *For Better or for Worse: Divorce Reconsidered.* New York: W. W. Norton and Company.

In addition to work previously described for each of these researchers, they both conclude the same thing. The thousands of children they have studied demonstrate that children in single, mother-headed households and children from divorced families do as well academically and have no greater behavior problems than their peers from both happy and unhappy intact families.

Chapter 12

Gabardi, Lisa, and Lee Rosen. (1992). "Intimate relationships: College students from divorced and intact families," *Journal of Divorce and Remarriage* 18 (3–4): 25–56.

Wallerstein, Judith; Julia Lewis; and Sandra Blakeslee. (2000). *The Unexpected Legacy of Divorce.* New York: Hyperion.

These are just two examples of the conflicting data on dating and sexual intimacy among young people from divorced families and outcomes for their own marriages later in life. The evidence seems to substantiate that children from divorced families can be somewhat more mistrustful and cautious about becoming deeply involved romantically. When they do become romantically involved, Gabardi and Rosen find they do so in numbers equal to the general population, they do not break up with any greater frequency, they do not act promiscuously more than their peers do, and they do not divorce more frequently in later life.

Chapter 13

Amato, Paul R.; Laura S. Loomis; and Alan Booth. (1995). "Parental divorce, marital conflict, and offspring well-being during early adulthood," *Social Forces* 73 (3): 895–916.

Amato conducted a 12-year longitudinal study of over two thousand divorced families. He reached and interviewed over 500 adult children who had grown up in those families. He and his colleagues found that the key to the adult children's psychological well being was the level of conflict between their parents when the children were growing up, not whether their parents remained married or got divorced. The greater and more lasting the conflict between their parents had been, the lower the level of psychological well being of the now grown children throughout their lifetimes. When children grew up in divorced families where conflict was minimized, they demonstrated increased emotional maturity a few years after their parents' divorce.

Chapter 14

Brinig, Margaret, and Douglas Allen. (2000). "These Boots Are Made for Walking: Why Most Divorce Filers are Women," *American Journal of Law and Economics* Vol 2: 126–169.

Brinig and Allen studied all 46,000 divorces filed in one year, 1995, in four states: Connecticut, Virginia, Montana, and Oregon, the only states that collect the information they sought. They found that women were more than twice as likely to file for divorce as men, and that afterwards women reported they were more often happier than their former husbands subsequent to divorce. Women in the study said they were much more willing to break up their marriages if they anticipated getting sole custody of their children, enabling them to gain control of the children. In states where joint custody was typically awarded, women described they were more reluctant to file for divorce.

Whoever filed for divorce (the husband or wife) in the four states studied tended to be the better educated spouse; in this study, it was most frequently the woman. The women who filed for divorce frequently indicated that a major reason for filing was that they had become bored with their husbands and saw them as failing to continue to advance themselves or grow. Abuse and adultery accounted for a relatively small percentage of the reasons for women seeking divorce.

Chapter 15

Stewart, Abigail, J., *et al.* (1997). *Separating Together: How Divorce Transforms Families.* New York: The Guilford Press.

Stewart's study also investigates financial repercussions comprehensively. She concludes that "evidence does not suggest that the economic implications of divorce, by themselves, should serve as a major deterrent to it." She reports that: 93 percent of women in her study remained in their homes; three quarters were employed outside the home when they separated. Eighty five percent of the divorces she studied were settled out of court. Two-thirds of the women in her study said their finances grew worse in the beginning of their separation or divorce. In contrast, however, most of these same women felt "the gains of personal financial autonomy . . . offset the losses in financial resources."

Index

About the Authors

Dr. Lawrence Birnbach is a psychoanalyst who specializes in working with individuals and couples in troubled relationships. He maintains private practices in New York City and Westport, Connecticut. He received his Ph.D. in psychology and his postdoctoral training certification in psychoanalysis, both from New York University. He has had a mental health column in the *Westport News*, and has published articles on divorce and relationships in journals and periodicals. He is a frequent speaker on these subjects.

Dr. Birnbach has been the chair of the training program at the Washington Square Institute, a psychoanalytic training institute in New York City, where he currently teaches on the faculty and serves as a training analyst and supervisor. He is the founder and director of the Master Class Supervision Series at Washington Square, a program that brings renowned psychoanalysts to the institute from all over the world. Dr. Birnbach has been an adjunct clinical professor in the NYU School Psychology program, and has worked as a school psychologist in the New York City and Westchester County schools. He serves on the boards of professional organizations as well as the Bidwell House Museum, a colonial museum in rural Massachusetts.

Dr. Beverly Hyman is president of an internationally known business and organizational consultancy specializing in conflict management, executive coaching, interpersonal communications, leadership, and organizational development. As a consultant to several United Nations agencies, she is involved in addressing the concerns of women and families. She is a frequent speaker at national and international conferences such as the UN Decade Conference for Women and the National Human Resources Conference. She has also chaired the Day of the International Woman at the United Nations. Other clients include the Metropolitan Museum of Art, Deutsche Bank, and Standard & Poor's. Her Ph.D. is from New York University's program in Culture and Communication. Dr. Hyman has published two business books and numerous articles in business journals and popular periodicals. She is Chair of the Dean's Council at New York University's Steinhardt School of Culture, Education, and Human Development. In 2003, she was the school's Alumna of the Year, and in 2008 NYU awarded her the university's Meritorious Service Award.

The authors, each of whom has one daughter from a prior marriage, were married to each other in 1997. They live in New York City and in the Berkshires in Massachusetts. Their daughters, son-in-law, and treasured granddaughter reside near them in New York City.

For more information, please visit www.bevandlarry.com